JOHNNY CASH

JOHNNY CASH

Frank Moriarty

MetroBooks

MetroBooks

An Imprint of Friedman/Fairfax Publishers

Library of Congress Cataloging-in-Publication Data

Moriarty, Frank.
        Johnny Cash   /   by Frank Moriarty.
                    p.   cm.
        Includes bibliographical references and index.
        ISBN 1-56799-488-1 (hc)
        1. Cash, Johnny.   2. Country musicians—United States—Biography.
I. Title.
ML420.C265M67   1997
782.421642'092—dc21
[B]   97-13034

Editor: Stephen Slaybaugh
Art Director: Jeff Batzli
Designer: Garrett Schuh
Photography Editor: Amy Talluto
Production Director: Karen Matsu Greenberg

Color separations by Ad. ver. srl.
Printed in Singapore by KHL Printing Co. Pte. Ltd.

1 3 5 7 9 10 8 6 4 2

For bulk purchases and special sales, please contact:
Friedman/Fairfax Publishers
Attention: Sales Department
15 West 26th Street
New York, NY 10010
212/685-6610 FAX 212/685-1307

Visit our website:
http://www.metrobooks.com

Dedication

This book is dedicated with love to my wife Portia, who has made the abrupt and disorienting musical transition from my last book—about Jimi Hendrix—to this book about Johnny Cash. Thanks for your enthusiasm, ideas, and support.

Acknowledgments

Thanks to the Michael Friedman Publishing Group for the opportunity to work on this project, and to my editor, Stephen Slaybaugh, for being such a pleasure to work with. Thanks to John L. Smith for assisting me with information on his exhaustive Johnny Cash discographies and release catalogs, and to American Recordings for their assistance with documenting the most recent phase of the career of Johnny Cash. Thanks to Rich Buckland at Bruce the Cat Productions in Yonkers, New York, for being such an excellent and reliable source for the massive Bear Family Records box sets spanning the career of Johnny Cash.

And finally, thanks to Richard Weize and Bear Family Records of Hambergen, Germany. Through the work of Richard and others at Bear Family, the recorded works of some of America's greatest artists are documented, collected, and made available to listeners all over the world. For the work with not only Johnny Cash, but many other musicians like Jerry Lee Lewis, Webb Pierce, Faron Young, Duane Eddy, Bill Haley, Carl Perkins, Hank Snow, and Ernest Tubb—thank you!

CONTENTS

CHAPTER 1

DELTA ROOTS

"Hello, I'm Johnny Cash."

Those four words have become part of the musical culture of America, a trademark as recognizable as any corporate logo or celebrity tag line.

Those words issue forth from a man dressed in black, armed only with an acoustic guitar and an incredible catalog of songs that define the very heart of his country. And there is ample proof of the connection that listeners feel with this man and his songs.

Just consider the more than one hundred Johnny Cash songs that have climbed the charts—and earned him numerous Grammy awards—during a career that has spanned more than four decades and is still going strong.

Simply put, Johnny Cash is the voice of the United States. And much like the nation is one of diversity, the subjects of Cash's songs are many and varied. The Man in Black, as he is often called, has offered plainspoken pledges of devotion, such as "I Walk The Line." He's expressed the gut-level consequences of misdeeds, in "Folsom Prison Blues." He has portrayed the brutal justice of early frontier America, in "25 Minutes to Go." And he's narrated true events that have shaped his nation in songs such as "Mr. Garfield."

Like the topics of his music, the life of Johnny Cash is a complex one. While vacuous personalities so often dwell in the realm of celebrity, Cash seems to live only in the real world—his hard origins and the troubles he has lived through and dealt with have flavored his art and made its impact all the greater. Johnny Cash is a musical legend, and his status continues to grow with each new recording.

Like many legends, the story of Johnny Cash has its roots in humble origins.

Kingsland, Arkansas is a tiny town right in the middle of the southern half of the state, 35 miles (56.3km) south of Pine Bluff and 70 miles (112.6km) south of Little Rock, the nearest big cities. It was here that John R. Cash was born, on February 26, 1932. Stardom awaited him 175 miles (281.6km) to the northeast in Memphis, Tennessee, but it would take Cash twenty-two years to travel that distance and meet his musical destiny. Until then, Johnny was known as J.R. or John.

Although John's family was poor, they were proud. His father, Ray Cash, the son of a Baptist minister and the youngest of twelve children in the continuation of a family that originally came to the United States from Scotland in 1673, was a World War I veteran who had fought in France. Ray and his wife, Carrie, saw to it that their offspring were raised as good Christian children, and their faith helped them through many hard times. Ray labored hard throughout the Depression, toiling in sawmills and working for the railroad. His wages, along with modest crops and livestock the family was able to maintain, kept the Cash mouths fed and even helped provide sustenance to some neighboring families who were worse off. Welfare or handouts were never accepted by the Cash family.

PAGES 8–9 : *John R. Cash at the beginning of his career, with a tale to tell and a Gibson guitar.* ABOVE: *Johnny poses with his mother, Carrie, in full rockabilly attire as the first signs of success were becoming apparent at Sun Records.* OPPOSITE: *Cash revisited the town of his birth with his friend, singer/songwriter Johnny Horton.*

Johnny Cash and Johnny Horton take a break in Kingsland, Arkansas from the grueling concert appearance schedule that characterized the country music life of the 1950s and 1960s.

Ray and Carrie Cash already had two sons, Roy and Jack, and a daughter, Louise, when John was born. The arrival of John's younger sister, Reba, came just before the first major move of Cash's young life. In February 1935 President Roosevelt's "New Deal" and the promise of a better life in a government-sponsored farming commu-

nity led the Cash clan to pack up and move out of Kingsland. They left behind the hill country in favor of the rich cotton lands of the delta region that parallels the storied Mississippi River. Their destination was Dyess, Arkansas, a 14,000-acre (5,656-hectare) parcel of cotton production 30 miles (48.3km) northwest of Memphis.

In his biography for the American Recordings label, Johnny Cash recalled that by the time he was three years old the guitar was already an important part of his life. His mother played the instrument, and the guitar made the move with the family from Kingsland to Dyess:

> *The guitar had come with us in the back of a moving truck from the hills of southern Arkansas to the flat black delta land of Mississippi county in the northeastern part of the state. It was February 1935 and I was three years old.*
>
> *The entire family, my parents, two brothers and two sisters, spent the first night in the truck under a tarpaulin. A cold rain fell all night, and the last thing I remember before going to sleep was my mother beating time on an old Sears-Roebuck guitar, singing "What Would You Give in Exchange for Your Soul."*
>
> *Earliest memories of our new home in the Delta revolve around my mother and that guitar. My father literally carved our new home out of twenty acres [8.1 hectares] of jungle with the help of one mule, my older brother, and the muscles in his arms. At night, on the front porch where we always gathered, I could hear panthers scream in the woods around us, but my mother's guitar and singing was like the harp of King David that we read about in the Bible. It brought a closeness and comfort that couldn't be found any other way.*

Some of those very same songs that John's mother sang to him would one day become mainstays of his own repertoire, as Cash came to recognize the timeless value of tunes like "Wreck of the Old 97."

Dyess was not a booming metropolis by any means. Consisting of sixteen numbered roads that ran through the town, Dyess boasted little more than a cannery, a general store, a service station, a small theater, a café, and the Road Fifteen Church of God. It was in the village church that John's exposure to musical instruments continued, as the pastor and the congregation welcomed a variety of guitars, mandolins, and banjos in the service of praising God.

The introduction into the Cash household of the small luxury of a radio from Sears, Roebuck also had a profound effect on John, as he listened to both church and country music programs on the big radio stations transmitting from Texas, Tennessee, and West Virginia—as long as the radio's batteries lasted, that is, for the Cash household was still without electricity.

John had grown closer to his older brother Jack as he grew toward his teenage years. Jack wanted to become a preacher, and seemed destined to fulfill that vision with his knowledge of the Bible and his strong faith. Not surprisingly, the two shared in church activities, but they also had their share

John with his brother Jack (right), whose death in 1944 had a profound impact on John's young life.

of childish exploits, such as selling watermelons to raise money to go see movies or toying with cottonmouth snakes sunning themselves by the banks of drainage ditches around Dyess.

It was a tremendous shock for John when, on May 12, 1944, Jack was terribly injured at his weekend job cutting fence posts. Jack was pulled into a swinging saw and maimed by the machine, suffering critical injuries. He clung to life for eight days, but his injuries were beyond the skills of the hospital doctors. Gangrene set in after a week, and Jack passed away the next day. Just before he died, however, Jack awoke and told his mother of a vision: he was going down a river, with fire on one side and heaven on the other; the singing of angels, he said, was guiding him to heaven.

His brother's death and the vision of heaven had a profound effect on John. Throughout the summer of 1944, as the world was torn by the war in Europe, the family grieved for their lost son and brother. But when a family livelihood depends on the harvesting of nature's bounty, work can never come to a stop for long. The young Cash children, out of school for the summer, labored together to make the family's cotton-raising efforts successful.

As time passed, John became close to his sister Reba, who was two years younger than he was; the two often sang as they worked together in the fields. John maintained his fascination with all the songs he heard on the radio, recreating the tunes he had heard and memorized as they hoed the earth beneath the hot Arkansas summer sun. From the radio, Cash absorbed music ranging from the country strains of Gene Autry and the Chuck Wagon Gang to the earthy sounds of Delta blues singers.

John's favorite radio program, *High Noon Roundup*, was broadcast daily from 12:30 to 1:00 P.M. on Memphis' influential WMPS. This half-hour variety show was hosted by Smilin' Eddie Hill and featured Ira and Charlie Louvin (the Louvin Brothers). Although John loved the *Roundup*, he loved the fifteen minutes that followed even more. This was when Hill and the Louvin Brothers reinvented themselves as the Lonesome Valley Trio. The threesome performed nothing but straight gospel, and John soaked in the influences they provided as often as he could.

So it should come as no surprise that one of the greatest thrills in the life of young John Cash came in early 1947 when he heard Hill announce over the radio that the *High Noon Roundup* gang was going to be performing a concert at Dyess High School. John Cash was the first to arrive at this show and the last to leave—he even met Charlie Louvin briefly in the afternoon and got a wave goodbye from the star as his car headed off toward Memphis in the post-concert darkness.

Seeing the *High Noon Roundup* performance had been everything John had hoped it would be and, if his mind hadn't been made up before, it was now—someday he would join his musical heroes and sing songs on the radio.

ABOVE: *Johnny Cash shakes hands with Eddie Hill, whose* High Noon Roundup *radio show in Memphis influenced Cash's decision to make music his life.* OPPOSITE: *One of Johnny Cash's earliest publicity photos, before his personal preference in clothing led to the nickname "The Man in Black."*

CHAPTER 2

JOHN CASH

MEETS THE TENNESSEE TWO

At fifteen years old,

John Cash knew what he wanted

to do—add his voice to the sounds

carried on the radio airwaves.

There was just one problem—Cash no

longer had access to a guitar, as he recalled decades later.

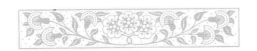

When I was eleven or twelve my mother's guitar mysteriously disappeared. I knew better than to ask if it had been sold to buy food and clothing for the family, and for all my young life the guitar wasn't mentioned again.

But I had a friend named Jesse Barnhill who lived three miles [4.8km] farther down the road. Jesse had had polio and his right hand and foot were withered, but with his left hand he made the chords as he beat a perfect rhythm with his tiny right hand. It was an old Gibson flattop, and I thought if I could play the guitar like that I'd sing on the radio some day.

I was at Jesse's house every afternoon after school and stayed until long after dark, singing along with him, or singing to his playing Hank Snow, Ernest Tubb, Jimmie Rodgers songs. Jesse taught me my first chord on the guitar, but my hands being too small, I didn't really learn to play then.

The long walk home alone at night was scary. It was pitch dark on the gravel road, and if the moon was shining, the shadows were even scarier. The panthers sounded closer and I just knew that every dark spot on the road was a cottonmouth snake ready to kill me.

But I sang all the way home, songs Jesse and I had been singing, and with the imaginary sound of the Gibson acoustic, I sang through the dark and decided that that kind of music was going to be my magic to take me through all the dark places.

In 1948, at the age of sixteen, as John's adolescence came to an end, his voice went through a sudden change. What had been a high, clear tenor voice suddenly changed to a deep, low-pitched rumble. Cash's voice had developed a tone that would fascinate listeners in the decades to come and become perhaps the most instantly recognizable voice of any singer ever.

But listeners and fans were still in the future in 1950, when, at the age of eighteen, John Cash enlisted in the United States Air Force. Cash had made a brief sojourn north to Detroit, following tales of good jobs available in the auto industry. But he was miserable in Michigan, and soon returned home with no prospects for the future. He hoped that the air force would give him direction.

As has been the case with many other musicians, service in the armed forces exposed John Cash not only to more of the world than he had ever seen, but also to more fellow musicians.

Stationed in Germany, Cash bought his first guitar for twenty marks (roughly five dollars). This guitar was an instrument of such suspect origins that it didn't even have a name on the headstock. But while others in the service seemed to be using all their time off to drink as much as possible, Cash focused on playing music with his new friends. The jam sessions, which included dips into the songbooks of artists like Hank Williams and the Carter Family, would often wrap up with a run through a host of gospel songs. It was comforting to be playing music from home while stationed thousands of miles from Arkansas.

In one of his earliest record company biographies, Johnny Cash recalled sharing some of his music from home for an appreciative audience in Italy.

On a vacation to Italy from our base in Germany, Ted Freeman and I were in one of the sidewalk cafes in Venice. The Italians are great lovers of music, and at many of the cafes, guitarists and violinists are playing constantly. Ted and I sat and listened, then, after we felt we were welcome there, asked for the guitars to play. Ted played lead on one guitar and I played and sang with the other. Before long, we had a crowd of about 300 around, and the restaurant owner insisted that we play on, because we had brought in so much business for him. And although we played songs they didn't understand, they seemed to enjoy it. We spoke no Italian, and

PAGES 16-17: *Signed to Sun Records and ready to rock—Luther Perkins, John Cash, and Marshall Grant (left to right).* OPPOSITE: *Sun Records struck gold with Elvis Presley, so it was only natural that Sun boss Sam Phillips would encourage Cash to present a similar image.*

Johnny Cash's unique voice, with its rumbling depth, was unlike any other on the pop charts.

they spoke no English, they requested songs for us to play by humming parts of country songs they had heard on the American Forces Network. After three or four hours we left them, and they seemed to have enjoyed the good old country songs.

Despite his initial abstinence, Cash eventually began drinking beer in Germany. From beer, he stepped up to cognac. For the first

time in his young life, he began to try out curse words in his conversations. By his third year in the air force, Cash was spending his free time with the drinking crowd, occasionally topping off the drinking with a brawl or two.

When he wasn't carousing with his buddies, Cash was slowly developing his musical abilities. He had bought a tape recorder to go along with his guitar, and he spent hours recording the songs he was now writing. He also formed an acoustic band, which he dubbed The Barbarians, adding two other acoustic guitars and a mandolin to complement his own flourishing guitar style. The Barbarians played a string of bars in the German equivalent of the honky tonk circuit. Sets ended either when the clubs closed or when The Barbarians became too drunk to continue playing.

During his time in the air force, Cash received a scar on his cheek that served to enhance his tough appearance. But, legends to the contrary, the scar didn't come from the blade of a knife during a knock-down, drag-out bar fight. Instead, the wound came at the hand of an inebriated German doctor botching a cyst removal.

On July 4, 1954, Staff Sergeant John Cash received an honorable discharge from the U.S. Air Force at Camp Kilmer, New Jersey. Soon after, there was another big change in Cash's life—marriage to Vivian Liberto.

Cash had met Vivian in Texas while undergoing air force training at the Lackland base just after enlisting—he had literally run into her when both were rollerskating at a rink in San Antonio. John had corresponded with Vivian while in the service, and despite the potential religious conflicts of her Catholicism and his Baptist background, the two were married on August 7, 1954, at St. Ann's Catholic Church in San Antonio.

Immediately after they were married, Cash and his bride settled in Memphis, where John's brother Roy also lived. John had decided that the best way to break into the music business was as a disc jockey, and he enrolled in a course financed by the GI Bill to study radio announcing at Keegan's School of Broadcasting in Memphis. But Cash was now a married man, and soon there was a baby on the way, so he was forced to earn a more mundane living selling appliances for the Home Equipment Company while he studied part-time.

A rare quiet moment as Cash's career gains momentum. Johnny tends to some guitar maintenance under the watchful eye of wife Vivian.

Roy Cash had risen to the post of night service manager at the Automotive Sales Garage in Memphis. Knowing of his brother's continuing obsession with music, Roy decided that John should meet Marshall Grant and Luther Perkins, two of the garage's mechanics who also played music in their spare time. What Roy couldn't have known was that he had just set the lineup of one of the most important and influential country/rockabilly groups of the 1950s—Johnny Cash and the Tennessee Two.

Luther Perkins was born in Memphis on January 8, 1928. His father was driving a taxi at the time, but the family soon returned to farming in Mississippi. As a nine-year-old, Luther dreamed of a pot of gold at the end of a rainbow. When he woke up, he knew right where he had to go to find the spot where the rainbow had touched down. With his brother in tow, Luther went to that location and dug. They found the remains of an old house and, after unearthing as many bricks as possible, Luther sold the materials to a construction company for two cents each. With the nine dollars he raised in proceeds, Luther bought his first guitar.

Marshall Grant, Perkins' music and mechanics partner, came from the tiny hamlet of Flatts, North Carolina. Along with his eleven brothers and sisters, Grant was raised on a twenty-acre (8.1-hectare) tract of land in the middle of the Smoky Mountains. But the Grant family, like the Cash clan, was lured from the mountains by cotton. They moved near Bessamer City and share-cropped as best they could.

In time, however, Grant tired of that life and joined his brother in Memphis, where, at the age of nineteen, he met and married his wife, Etta, and learned the trade of automotive repair. It was only when he landed the job at Automotive Sales that he met Luther. Luther and Marshall used to jam in the washroom at Automotive Sales when things were slow, but for their first session with Cash they went to Luther's home on Nathan Street in Memphis. Among the songs they tried out the first time they got together was Hank Snow's "Moving On."

The three men found that they got along well, and so they continued to get together on an informal basis. Luther and Marshall, however, differed from John in one important respect—they were happy with their salaries as mechanics and had no interest in music as a profession. John, however, was miserable selling appliances. Even if he was able to eke out a living for his family, selling vacuum cleaners, washing machines, and refrigerators left him disheartened. His childhood dream of singing his songs on stage and having his music played on the radio still burned as brightly as it had when he was a teenager.

One night, when Cash got together with Perkins and Grant, he suggested that the threesome try some instruments other than the three ordinary acoustic guitars they had used up to this point. Luther borrowed an electric guitar to complement John's cheap-but-reliable German guitar, and it was left to Marshall to borrow an upright bass.

Once Marshall had procured the massive instrument, there was a new problem—how to tune and play it. Luther wound up playing notes on his guitar, which Marshall matched on the fretless bass neck and then marked with tape. Despite the bass' tendency to go out of tune in mid-song, Marshall eventually wound up buying the instrument for seventy-five dollars.

Soon the three began to play more seriously. All of the men were self-taught musicians, and long hours of practice brought the group's skill levels higher and higher. Cash was following a path toward his goal of a professional music career and, whether they could see it happening or not, Luther and Marshall were now solidly along for the ride.

As 1954 wore on, Cash and his two friends played for audiences for the first time. And the more they played, the more distressed John became with his work situation. Finally, his boss, George Bates, asked him what he really wanted to do. It didn't take much prodding to get Cash to tell the truth.

By the end of the conversation, George Bates had agreed to pay fifteen dollars a week to sponsor Cash as he performed on his own fifteen-minute radio show on country station KWEM every Saturday afternoon

ABOVE: *Johnny Cash is all smiles in this publicity photo.* OPPOSITE: *But the reality of life as a country music star is more accurately reflected here, as a serious Cash waits to record a session.*

ABOVE: *Guitarist Luther Perkins (left) and bassist Marshall Grant reap the rewards of leaving the automotive repair life behind to go with Cash. Here The Tennessee Two receive the "Best New Instrumental Group" award from* Jamboree *in November 1957.* RIGHT: *Johnny Cash and the Tennessee Three. The rhythm section of Marshall Grant and drummer W.S. Holland look across the stage to guitarist Luther Perkins as Cash grins at center.*

at two o'clock. Finally, the songs of John Cash would be heard on the radio.

Before the first show could even begin, Marshall Grant had to overcome a nearly paralyzing case of stage fright. He succeeded, and Luther, John, and Marshall's brief initial foray into weekly radio fame lasted about two months. Between songs John would deliver the commercials for Home Equipment.

Although the radio show didn't exactly become a Memphis institution, it did build confidence in the three young men as to what they were capable of musically. And the show helped bring in more performance bookings in the region.

With things progressing at such a steady pace, it seemed inevitable that John Cash and the Tennessee Two would want to try making a record. And in Memphis in 1954, everybody knew where to go to do that—Sam Phillips' Sun Record Company.

CHAPTER 3

STARDOM

AT SUN

The address: 706 Union Avenue,

Memphis, Tennessee.

The importance: ground zero of a

musical explosion that shook the world

of popular music to its very core—the

location of Sun Studio and the headquarters

of Sam Phillips' ground-breaking record label,

Sun Record Company.

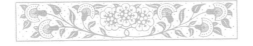

It was from this small building that some of the most important rock and roll records came, and it was to this address that John Cash went to stake his claim to fame.

By the time Cash and the Tennessee Two decided to record their tunes, Sam Phillips had already recorded a number of soon-to-be legendary blues stars, including B.B. King and Howlin' Wolf, for other record labels. But it had dawned on Sam that his profits could skyrocket if he released his own records on his own label. So in February 1952 he approached Nashville label owner Jim Bulleit for startup funds, and thus was born the Sun Record Company.

With Sam's brother, Judd, acting in the capacity of promotion director, the two set about the task of establishing their fledgling label. It took until April 1953 for Sun to score a hit record: Rufus Thomas' "Bear Cat"—a musical reply to the then-hot "Hound Dog" as recorded by Willie Mae Thornton—soared to number three on the rhythm and blues (R&B) charts and delivered the first solid seller for Phillips.

Sam soon began recording and releasing a string of records by local R&B singers. Phillips was a shrewd businessman, and went to such publicity-generating lengths as to sign the Prisonaires—five felons confined at the Nashville State Penitentiary who were allowed to record in Memphis only while surrounded by armed guards. Phillips was also well aware of the passion for R&B music that was growing among white Southern teenagers. He often mused aloud that if he could just find that one white kid with "the Negro sound," his ship would come in. And then, in mid-1953, Elvis Presley sauntered through the doors of Sun Records to record a song for his mother's birthday.

It took months for Sam and Elvis to get hooked up and for the right sound to be dialed in, but finally, in July 1954, one of the truly epochal recording sessions of all time took place—and Sam Phillips had one big star on his hands. As Elvis' star ascended, so did the reputation of Sun Records. Soon Sam Phillips had his hands full with would-be rockers determined to follow in Elvis' mighty footsteps—and John Cash was one of those in line for a ticket to stardom.

Cash had an "in" at Sun, for he had met Elvis' guitarist, Scotty Moore. When John asked for the best route to a Sun audition, Scotty gave him the simplest of directions—just keep showing up at the studio.

PAGES 16-17: *Johnny Cash poses with the Brothers Four as producer Sam Katzman listens in.* ABOVE: *The humble exterior of the building that changed the face of popular music: headquarters of Sam Phillips' Sun Record Company and its legendary recording studio.*

The building found at that address is almost nondescript, tucked into the middle of a block in central Memphis. But from within the tiny confines of its main recording room came a sound so big that it influenced everyone from The Beatles to Led Zeppelin to Jimi Hendrix.

Johnny Cash in the studio, polishing a lyric before recording the tune to tape for posterity.

In 1954 John Cash strode beneath the sign over the door that read, "THE MEMPHIS RECORDING SERVICE—Combining the NEWEST and BEST EQUIPMENT with the latest and FINEST SONOCOUSTIC STUDIOS." Rest assured that the only dictionary containing the word "sonocoustic" resided in the mind of Sam Phillips.

Although it was easy to get in Sun's front door, Cash found it harder to get to Phillips. He tried numerous times, sometimes well aware that Sam was in fact in the building when he was told that the producer was out. But John persisted, and one day Phillips gave him a listen.

Cash must have been elated when he was told to return with his band for a more formal audition. Armed with the Tennessee Two and with steel guitar player Red Kernodle in tow, Cash returned to Sun Studio. Unfortunately, the gospel repertoire Cash and company presented for Phillips left Sam unimpressed. What else did they have?

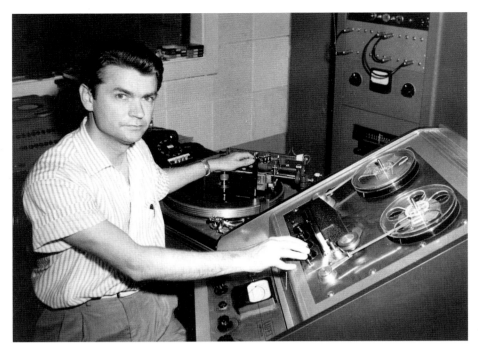

Sam Phillips mans the tape reels. It was Phillips' ear for talent that revolutionized rock and roll, as Sam saw the potential of Presley, Cash, Jerry Lee Lewis, Carl Perkins, and a host of others.

In a 1950s Sun biography, Cash recalled what happened next:

> *For days I thought about it and tried to figure out, "What would be different?" The only good idea I had was part of a poem that I had written on my way home from overseas. I finished the poem, put a tune to it and Luther and Marshall and I got together and played it over and over until it sounded right. The name of the song was "Hey Porter." When I went back to Sun the next time, Marshall and Luther went with me, and Mr. Phillips recorded it the second time we played it. I practically flew home to Vivian.*

Actually, Phillips sent Cash, Perkins, and Grant away with a request that they come up with another tune like "Hey Porter"—but it was a start with real promise. And Eddie Hill, whose *High Noon Roundup* had had such a profound influence on young John Cash, also played a role in the development of the flip-side of "Hey Porter." In the same Sun Records biography, Cash recalled how this came to be:

Eddie now was a disc jockey on WSM, Nashville, Tennessee, the home of the Grand Ole Opry. One night while listening to him, I heard him say, as he said nearly every night, "Stay tuned, we're gonna bawl, squall, and run up the wall." Somehow the words stuck with me. The next day at work I kept saying them over and over to myself. I decided that a good idea for a novelty song would be "You're gonna Bawl, Bawl, Bawl." I started writing it, but I didn't like it. I decided to make it a serious song instead of a novelty, and called it, "You're gonna Cry, Cry, Cry." When the record was released on June 26, 1955, it was called just "Cry, Cry, Cry." But there was no crying going on. It was one of the happiest days of my life.

Still, it took a frustrating period of months—with recording sessions taking place in March and May of 1955—before Sam Phillips was ready to release the first Johnny Cash single. Sun Records catalog number 221, "Hey Porter" backed with "Cry, Cry, Cry," was finally issued in June 1955. Up to this time known as plain old John, Cash was told by Sam Phillips to start going by the sportier version of his name, Johnny, and Luther and Marshall were officially dubbed the Tennessee Two.

While waiting for the single to be released, the threesome had taken such prestigious gigs as standing on a truck's flatbed, advertising an auto sale as they played for four hours to pick up $50. Things had to get better soon—Johnny and Vivian's daughter, Rosanne (who later added the "e" to her name), had been born on May 24.

Eventually, the first Johnny Cash single would sell roughly a hundred thousand copies, but Johnny's first Sun Record Company royalty check was for the miniscule amount of $2.41. Nevertheless, Johnny was confident that more would soon be coming in.

Thanks to Sam Phillips' recording vision, Johnny was right. Sam realized that Cash had a sound unlike any of the would-be rockabilly cats who streamed in Sun's front door, and he worked at complementing that unique sound. Phillips' goal was to keep the Cash recordings stark, with the vocals solidly placed in the middle of the mix. Luther's reserved guitar style just added to the evocative loneliness of the recordings' overall feel, and Phillips' crowning touch was the "slapback" echo

Two of the big guns who put Sun Records on the musical map: Johnny Cash and Elvis Presley, pictured in 1957.

and reverb that thickened up the sound without clouding the simple elements of the performances. It was a winning combination, and one that Cash came to rely on for his entire career.

But in 1955 that career consisted mostly of Johnny's somewhat desperate attempts at self-promotion. Determined to make a living singing, Cash had given up his radio schooling to drive throughout southwestern Tennessee and the neighboring counties, trying to book performances at theaters and schoolhouses. As insurance, he hung onto his sales job; Luther and Marshall, meanwhile, were still turning wrenches to feed their families. Johnny Cash and the Tennessee Two made anywhere from six to fifty dollars for these early forays onto the stage, but at least Cash was headlining. And the people seemed to really like what they saw on stage and were finally beginning to hear on the radio.

Eventually, "Hey Porter" and "Cry, Cry, Cry" made it to number fourteen on the country charts. Never one to rush into anything, Sam Phillips had held off on another Cash recording session at Sun until he'd had enough time to assess the performance of the first single. Now he was ready: in December 1955 Phillips finally issued the second Cash single, containing what has become one of Johnny Cash's signature songs: "Folsom Prison Blues," which was backed with the less remembered "So Doggone Lonesome." Phillips splurged with an advertisement for the single in music trade papers.

Meanwhile, Johnny and the Tennessee Two had roamed farther from home than ever. On December 28 they journeyed all the way down to Texarkana, at the border of Arkansas and Texas, to play a date with a young singer named George Jones. Earlier in the month they had guested on the highly influential country music radio show *Louisiana Hayride*; they went over so well that they were offered a regular slot on the show as 1956 began. Every Saturday night the band burned a trail from Memphis to Shreveport, gaining priceless commercial exposure with each broadcast. With this success, Johnny Cash finally quit his job at Home Equipment. The days of selling appliances had, mercifully, come to an end.

Battling "Folsom Prison Blues" on the charts was a song by yet another Sam Phillips discovery: Carl Perkins' "Blue Suede Shoes." The success of this song rivaled Cash's performance on the country charts, but Perkins did Cash one better—his hit also crossed over onto the pop charts. Professional competition aside, Johnny Cash and Carl Perkins, who had met in the summer of 1955, became close friends. Perkins even played a role in the birth of what was to be Johnny Cash's biggest hit yet.

The song was "I Walk the Line," and the story of its creation is so strange and unlikely that one could be forgiven for thinking that it must be fiction.

The tale begins with Johnny Cash's little tape recorder back in the air force days. Cash returned from duty one night, noticed that some-

OPPOSITE: *Although he has written lighthearted songs like "One Piece at a Time," Cash is usually remembered for tunes of a more sombre tone.*

ABOVE: *A young Johnny Cash hits the concert trail, playing songs from his sessions at Sun.*

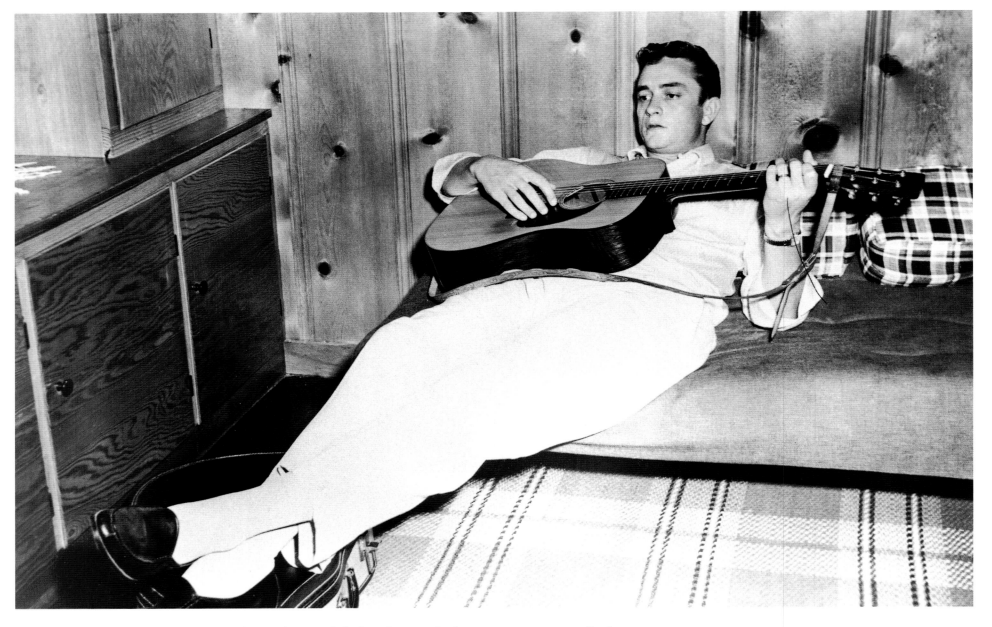

In a rather unusual Sun publicity photo, this candid shot depicts Cash in a rare moment of relaxation.

one had been playing around with the machine, and pressed the play button. He heard what sounded like the word "father" followed by a bizarre chord progression.

Cash began an investigation of the mysterious sounds, eventually determining that the reel-to-reel tape had been flipped over, recorded on, and then flipped yet again. What Cash had heard that night was the sound of guitar and a voice saying, "Turn it off"—but he heard it backwards. Regardless, Cash couldn't get the sounds of the eerie chords out of his mind.

Many years later, in 1956, while backstage at a show in Gladewater, Texas, Johnny Cash sat strumming through those very same chords as Carl Perkins sat nearby. Perkins' attention was captured by the unique sound, and the rockabilly master told Johnny he should incorporate those chords into a new song for Sam Phillips, as Sam was always looking for something that sounded different. The question was, what to call it.

When conversation turned to the temptations of life on the road, Cash mentioned that he would not play around—he would "walk the line." In his 1975 biography *Man In Black*, Cash wrote about what happened next:

> *"'I Walk the Line' would be a good title," Carl said.*
> *"Hmmmmmmmmm—" I began.*
> *The song came easily. It was one of those rare times I've felt a song was just "begging to be written." There was no wringing the mind or biting the pencil on "I Walk the Line." The lyrics came as fast as I could write, and in twenty minutes I had it finished.*

Johnny Cash and the Tennessee Two returned to Sun Studio on April 2, 1956, to record "I Walk the Line." The second recorded take became the version released as Sun Records catalog number 241, backed by the propulsive "Get Rhythm."

"I Walk the Line" didn't walk when it was released in May—it ran up the charts, all the way to number two on the country charts and number nineteen on the pop charts. At last Cash had a crossover hit, much to Sam Phillips' pleasure.

To this day, "I Walk the Line" remains one of the most unique singles ever released. Keeping the stark sonic aura that Phillips had perfected, the odd key changes only made the song stand out even more. Add to the mix Cash's voice, which sounded aged well beyond his twenty-four years, and Phillips had a song that made listeners take notice.

The same month that Johnny Cash's new single was released, he signed with Bob Neal's talent agency, Stars Inc. Neal had been a disc jockey in Memphis for many years, and with his star rising Cash needed representation by someone familiar with the music business.

Not that Cash's increasing popularity meant life was a bed of roses. Out on the road, John, Luther, and Marshall were surviving the worst the concert trail could dish out. Together, they were making from fifty to a hundred dollars per night, and this money had to go to support all three families. Often, the three had to drive all night after a show, and when the luxury of a cheap motel was indulged in there was a game of matching coins held to determine who got to sleep in a bed alone and who had to share.

"I don't really care to remember those first shows I played," Cash told Christopher Wren for the 1971 book *Winners Got Scars Too*. "It was new and exciting, and they would talk about playing Helena, Arkansas, which was a big deal then, but I knew there was something bigger ahead.

"Those shows aren't pleasant memories. They're not the good old days to me."

The road work was necessary because, by the end of 1957, Cash was the third best-selling country artist, behind Marty Robbins and Ray Price. A fourth Sun single had done well, and Johnny Cash and the Tennessee Two ranged far and wide as part of a number of "package" tours that gathered together numerous country stars.

It was in 1957, while on one of these seemingly endless treks, that Johnny Cash was exposed to one of the most common dangers of life on the road. Luther Perkins was at the wheel with Johnny by his side as

Sam Phillips' smile shows that Sun has once again struck gold, as he presents Cash with the Gold Record award for "I Walk the Line."

they drove late at night from a show in Miami to a show in Jacksonville, Florida. They were following singer Faron Young's car when the lead car pulled over. Luther followed suit. Gordon Terry, who had become friendly with Cash, was driving Young's car. Cash recounted what happened then in *Man In Black*:

> *"Are you sleepy, Luther?" Gordon asked.*
>
> *"I sure am," he said.*
>
> *"Take one of these. It'll keep you awake." And he gave Luther a little white pill with a cross on it.*
>
> *"What are they?" I asked Gordon.*
>
> *"Bennies," he said.*
>
> *"Will they hurt you?" I asked.*
>
> *"I don't think so," said Gordon. "They've never hurt me. Here, have one. They'll make you want to go to Jacksonville and enjoy yourself after you get there."*
>
> *I took one of the white pills and got in the car with Gordon. Within thirty minutes I felt refreshed, wide-awake, and talkative.*

In Jacksonville, Johnny Cash never did get to sleep. He simply took another pill before the show. He had discovered one of most common and potentially dangerous crutches that touring musicians have relied on for decades—amphetamines.

With artificial stimulation keeping the musicians going and appearances on such shows as Jackie Gleason's variety program and the Grand Ole Opry spurring demand, Cash toured as far west as California.

It was while he was in California in the summer of 1957 that Johnny Cash got an idea of just how far his popularity had spread: in Compton for an appearance on the Town Hall Party on August 31, Cash was approached by Columbia's Don Law, an influential British-born record label executive who headed Columbia's country & western division. It was to be the beginning of a long and productive relationship, as Law would oversee many of Cash's most important recordings in the years to come.

Law discreetly inquired if Cash might be persuaded to make a move to Columbia once his Sun commitment was fulfilled. Johnny

ABOVE: *In this Sun Records photograph, Cash smiles despite the presence of some ghostly guitar necks lurking over his shoulder.* OPPOSITE: *One of the earliest examples of the somber "The Man in Black" imagery, seen here in a Sun Records publicity photo.*

answered in the affirmative, although he still had a full year to go in his contract with Sam Phillips. Eventually, Cash would sign a secret agreement with Columbia in November 1957, although an official announcement of the signing would not come until several months later.

That night in August, Cash and the Tennessee Two were definitely up, putting on a wild show for the Town Hall Party that started off with a rock-and-roll cover of one of Elvis' hits.

"Thank you, thank you," Cash announced as he and the Tennessee Two took the stage.

Johnny Cash onstage with the Tennessee Two, enjoying the sounds coming from Luther Perkins' guitar amp as Marshall Grant's bass fills in the bottom.

"Friends, this time for our first song, we want to do you a little rock and roll song. Rock and roll is doing pretty well in the business now—as a matter of fact, it nearly is the business. And y'all have probably heard of Elvis Presley; he's doing pretty good, too. He's got a song on one of his albums that he had recorded that I thought would have been a pretty good hillbilly song. But he went on and recorded it his way and sold thirty or forty times as many records on it as we would. (laughs)

"But we'd like to kind of tear it up for you—I mean do it for you, and we hope you'll like the way we do it. It's just a little hillbilly arrangement on this tender little love song of his called 'Go Cat.'"

Then Cash restated the title, adding a California touch.

"'I've Got Me a Woman'—over in Pasadena. Go cat!"

The band then launched into a rollicking cover of the Presley hit "I Got a Woman," which was written by Ray Charles and had been released a year before in August 1956.

"Go cat, but watch where you go!" Cash cautioned in midsong as Luther stepped forward to offer one of his concise solos. As the song wound towards its blues-based conclusion, Cash joked with the audience.

"Y'all don't want to miss this last part here," Johnny said. "It's the best part of the whole song. And the reason it's so good is because it's close to the end! Ha!"

The wild response of the audience must have reassured Columbia's Law as to the wisdom of offering Cash a deal for the future.

Later in the show, Cash went into a series of very funny impersonations—imitating Hank Snow, recreating what a broken Ernest Tubb record might sound like, warbling in a bizarre falsetto as Kitty Wells, lampooning Elvis' "Heartbreak Hotel," and even roaring through a brief but wild parody of Little Richard's "Long Tall Sally." The segment was accompanied by much hysteria on the part of the crowd.

Clearly, Cash and the Tennessee Two were having as much fun as those who were paying to see them—and if that fun got some help in the form of a bottle of 100 pills that cost about eight or ten dollars, well that's what everybody else on the concert trail was doing, too.

While in California, Johnny Cash met the promoter who had booked the shows: Stewart Carnall. Carnall had first heard Cash when he happened to catch a jukebox playing "Hey Porter." He was so impressed by the sounds coming from the jukebox that he proceeded to track down manager Bob Neal on the phone that very same day. By the end of the phone call, Stew had booked Cash and the Tennessee Two for the ten-day tour of California.

At the conclusion of the tour, Carnall was so convinced of Johnny Cash's potential that he struck a deal with Neal to share representation. Carnall immediately changed how Cash was paid for concerts—instead of a flat fee, Cash now received a guaranteed minimum against a percentage of the total house proceeds.

Meanwhile, Cash had made an impression at the Grand Ole Opry and was invited to become a regular performer on the prestigious stage. Although playing at the Opry was an honor professionally, from a busi-

Sam Phillips performs some image adjustment to Johnny Cash's look in the period before Cash left Phillips' Sun Records label in 1958.

ness point of view it was questionable whether it was worth it or not. After all, it meant that each Saturday night Johnny Cash and the Tennessee Two were unavailable for other concerts; instead they were forced to travel to Nashville every week for the show—and they were only paid scale to boot. Eventually, in 1957, Cash gave up his Opry slot.

Cash, Perkins, and Grant were now on the road for eight months out of the year. While income from the shows had gone up, Johnny still had to pay all of the travel expenses as well as supporting his growing

Although record sales are important to reputations, artists make their real money by touring constantly. Johnny Cash has logged millions of miles along the concert trail.

family. Johnny and Vivian had had two more daughters, Kathy and Cindy, but at least they were now able to live in a house Johnny owned instead of the cramped apartments where the family had resided before royalties from the Sun hits had begun to come in.

Of course, spending most of the year on the road going from one two-shows-per-night gig to another frequently made home seem very far away. And the succession of pills and their false energy didn't help. By the end of 1957, Johnny, Luther, and Marshall were ready to come off the road for a spell.

In July 1957, Sam Phillips had turned over the creative production of Johnny's records to Jack Clement, Sun's other chief producer. After Sam helmed the August sessions for Johnny Cash's first long-playing record (LP) for Sun—scheduled for release in November—Clement sat in the producer's chair for the rest of Johnny's Sun sessions. Unlike the less-is-better approach of Sam Phillips, Clement wanted to move Johnny in a more musically dense, pop music direction.

The first single issued under Clement's direction, "Home of the Blues" backed with the western ballad "Give My Love to Rose," climbed to number five on the country charts. The response from listeners to the production touches added by Clement to "Home of the Blues," such as the piano and chorus vocals, encouraged him to continue beefing up Johnny's minimalist sound.

The next Jack Clement session took place on November 12, 1957, just days after the release of the colorfully titled Sun album *Johnny Cash and His Hot and Blue Guitar*. Clement's plan was to have Cash record a song that Jack himself had written: "Ballad of a Teenage Queen." It was an obvious attempt by Clement to target the volatile, but lucrative, teenage listener market.

Topped off by a wavering soprano echoing the song's melody, "Ballad of a Teenage Queen," released as Sun single 283, tells a saccharine tale of a beautiful girl in love with a guy working at a candy store. One day, however, Hollywood talent scouts come to town and steal the girl away for a film career. "Dream on, dream on, Teenage Queen, see you on the silver screen!" emotes the chorus of background vocals, but eventually Teenage Queen follows her heart and surrenders fame for life at the candy store.

This uncharacteristic Cash song did not even boast Luther's participation—Clement played the guitar part. The flip side of this record, "Big River," was a much more typical Johnny Cash song.

Of course, there's an old saying that there is no accounting for taste. Much to everyone's surprise—except Jack Clement, who merely sat back and gloated—"Ballad of a Teenage Queen" shot up the charts throughout January and February of 1958, eventually peaking at number sixteen on the pop charts and taking the top spot on the country charts. By the first half of 1958, "Teenage Queen" had sold a whopping 280,000 copies.

Although things now looked rosy for all involved, Sam Phillips had been hearing rumors of Cash's impending departure at the conclusion of his contract. Cash owed Sun some sessions, and Phillips was determined to make the most of them.

In April 1958, "Guess Things Happen That Way" and "Come In Stranger" were released as Sun single 295. This single became Cash's biggest hit for the Sun Record Company, moving more than 300,000 units in just three months.

Sam Phillips could definitely use the revenue generated by Johnny Cash, and losing him was going to hurt even more because of developments across the ocean. In May, the British press discovered that Jerry Lee Lewis—perhaps Sun's biggest star—had married his thirteen-year-old cousin. Suddenly, sales of Jerry Lee's wild hits virtually stopped. That made sales of Johnny Cash product even more important to the survival of Phillips' label.

For Johnny Cash, however, the Sun era was coming to an end. After the sessions that yielded "Guess Things Happen That Way," Cash entered Sun to record only three more times before his final session on July 17, 1958. With the Tennessee Two augmented by Billy Riley on guitar, J.M. Van Eaton on drums, and Charlie Rich on piano, Cash recorded his last four songs for Sun: "It's Just About Time," "I Forgot to Remember to Forget," "I Just Thought You'd Like to Know," and "Down the Street to 301."

At the end of the day—and for the last time as an artist signed to Sam Phillips' famed Sun Record Company—Johnny Cash walked out the door of 706 Union Avenue, Memphis, Tennessee.

MILLION DOLLAR QUARTET

One of the most legendary—and mysterious—gatherings in the history of pop music took place on December 4, 1956, at Sun Record Company—this was the day of the Million Dollar Quartet.

Carl Perkins had been recording his latest single for Sun, augmented by a new Sam Phillips protégé, Jerry Lee Lewis, on piano. Johnny Cash happened to stop by Sun that afternoon, and then Elvis Presley walked in the door. Perkins, Lewis, Cash, and Presley: the Million Dollar Quartet.

That a photo of the foursome singing around Sun's piano was published soon after in the *Memphis Press Scimitar* is one of the few things everyone agrees on, and it's also a fact that some of the day's proceedings were recorded. But who did what and when they did it has been one of rock and roll's greatest unsolved mysteries for more than forty years.

Johnny Cash has contradicted himself by stating that he both was and was not there at the time of the actual recordings. In his *Man In Black* biography he even states that the session happened in the summer of 1955, not in 1956. At various times, Cash has recalled singing on songs like "Blueberry Hill," "Will the Circle Be Unbroken," and "There Are Strange Things Happening Every Day," but none of those songs appear on albums like the forty-track *The Complete Million Dollar Session: December 4th, 1956*, released by Britain's Charly Records Ltd. in 1987.

Somewhat easier to document was a second gathering of Sun Records alumni that took place thirty years later. With Roy Orbison replacing the late Elvis Presley, this second version of the Million Dollar Quartet found Cash, Perkins, Lewis, and Orbison collaborating on ten songs for a record called *Class of '55*. Recorded at Sun Studio and the nearby American Studio, this enjoyable ten-song release featured the group singing a tribute to Elvis, "We Remember The King," before wrapping things up with "Big Train (From Memphis)," written by former Creedence Clearwater Revival leader John Fogerty.

CHAPTER 4

PAYING

THE PRICE OF FAME

On August 1, 1958,

Columbia Records proudly

announced that Johnny Cash

had joined its roster. By getting

Cash and manager Bob Neal to commit

to the label as early as November 1957,

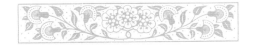

Columbia's Don Law had neatly avoided the potentially sticky situation of a record-label bidding war upon the expiration of Cash's Sun contract—interest in Cash had been high at other labels, particularly

ABOVE: *Johnny Cash concentrates in the studio at a session for his new record label.* PAGES 42–43: *Johnny Cash's performances in prisons would yield two of his most successful recordings for Columbia Records.*

at RCA Records. But Johnny Cash was impressed by the status that a contract with Columbia would give him, and the higher royalty rate that his new contract offered over his old Sun deal didn't hurt either.

Sam Phillips speculated that perhaps the root of Cash's defection was the possibility that Johnny was jealous of the attention that Phillips had lavished on his newest—and by now, in 1958, disgraced—star, Jerry Lee Lewis.

While the contract that bound Johnny Cash to Sun Records may have expired, the two names would be inexorably linked, not only historically, but commercially as well. Sam Phillips possessed the tapes of the sessions that Cash had rushed through in July 1958 when the Sun departure was imminent, and Phillips struck out at the Columbia deal by running an ad in the music trades containing an intriguing letter to retailers.

> *Johnny Cash began his musical career three years ago with Sun Records. In a comparatively short time, he has become a unique and distinctive artist occupying the #1 spot in his field...*
>
> *However, Johnny Cash signed with Columbia Records as of August 1, 1958. Upon learning that he was anticipating this move, we spent the next five months producing some of the finest sides for future Sun releases on Cash that we have ever had the pleasure of cutting.*
>
> *Please believe us when we say you are in for some tremendous releases on Cash on Sun for at least the next two years.*
>
> *Our thanks to Johnny for being a wonderful person to work with during our association. We are going to miss him to no end around 706 Union, but our aim is to keep him "hot" on Sun "If the Good Lord's Willing and the Creek Don't Rise."*
>
> *Appreciatively,*
> *Sam C. Phillips, President*
> *Sun Record Co.*

Phillips' threat to issue more Cash material was far from an idle one, and although his letter mentions releases for only two years, since the 1950s more than twenty-five full-length albums have been sewn

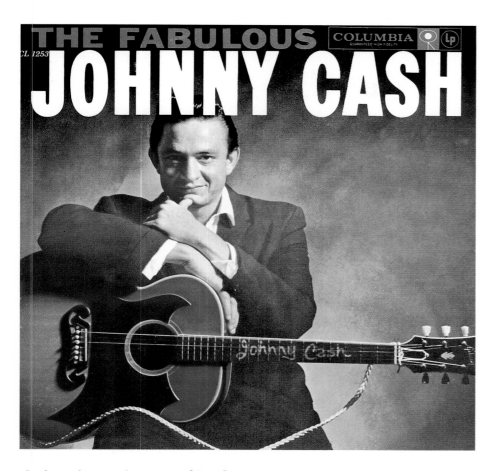

Cash smiles on the cover of his first Columbia album, looking confident that the label has the commercial power to help him move to the next level of stardom.

together in a myriad of combinations that mix the approximately seventy songs Cash recorded for Sun.

Johnny Cash wasted no time getting to work recording new material for Columbia. In fact, on July 24—a full week before the public announcement of the Columbia deal was made—he, Luther, and Marshall were ensconced in Nashville's Bradley Film & Recording Studio, with Don Law rolling the tapes as producer.

One of the songs Johnny Cash recorded that day, "It Was Jesus (Who Was It?)," pointed to one of the big differences between the Sun environment and the Columbia contract. Cash had always wanted to record gospel material, but Sam Phillips was strongly opposed to this inclination. Phillips wanted his artists targeting the charts, not fulfilling any religious ambitions. But when Cash had signed with Columbia, he got the go-ahead to go gospel in addition to recording more pop- and country-oriented material.

It was secular material, however, that made up *The Fabulous Johnny Cash*, his Columbia album debut released in November 1958. On the heels of Cash's first Columbia single—"All Over Again" backed with "What Do I Care" had reached number four on the country charts—the album rang up sales of more than 400 thousand units. And the next single, "Don't Take Your Guns to Town," claimed the top spot on the country charts and crossed over to number thirty-two on the pop charts. The flip side of this smash was "I Still Miss Someone."

Meanwhile, Johnny and his family had moved, along with manager Bob Neal, to Encino, California, in September. Neal was hoping to start a television program in California, and the potential for a film career for Johnny Cash offered additional incentive for the move.

While Luther and Marshall also took a good look at California as a potential home, they eventually decided to stick with Tennessee. There was really no benefit to physical proximity to the Johnny Cash living quarters, as Perkins and Grant could just as easily meet up with Cash at the first date of any concert tour.

Cash logged more television time throughout 1959, both with musical appearances on variety shows and in short dramatic turns on westerns like *Wagon Train*. The finances of the concert trail were also good to Cash in 1959, with a gross of 250 thousand dollars. Cash had even played in Australia in April and Britain in September, although the British shows were without Luther and Marshall due to strict musician union rules. Back in the United States, shows by Johnny Cash were selling out well in advance.

Of course, all this was coming at a price, and that was a growing dependence on chemical stimulants. Johnny himself wrote of the cost in *Man In Black*:

> *At times when I first began using them, I honestly believed the bennies were God-sent to help me be a better performer. My energy was multiplied. My timing was superb. I enjoyed every song in every concert and could perform with a driving, relentless intensity. They stimulated the mind, made me think faster and talk more.*
>
> *If I'd ever been shy before an audience, I wasn't any more. I rattled off my lines of dialogue between songs that kept people*

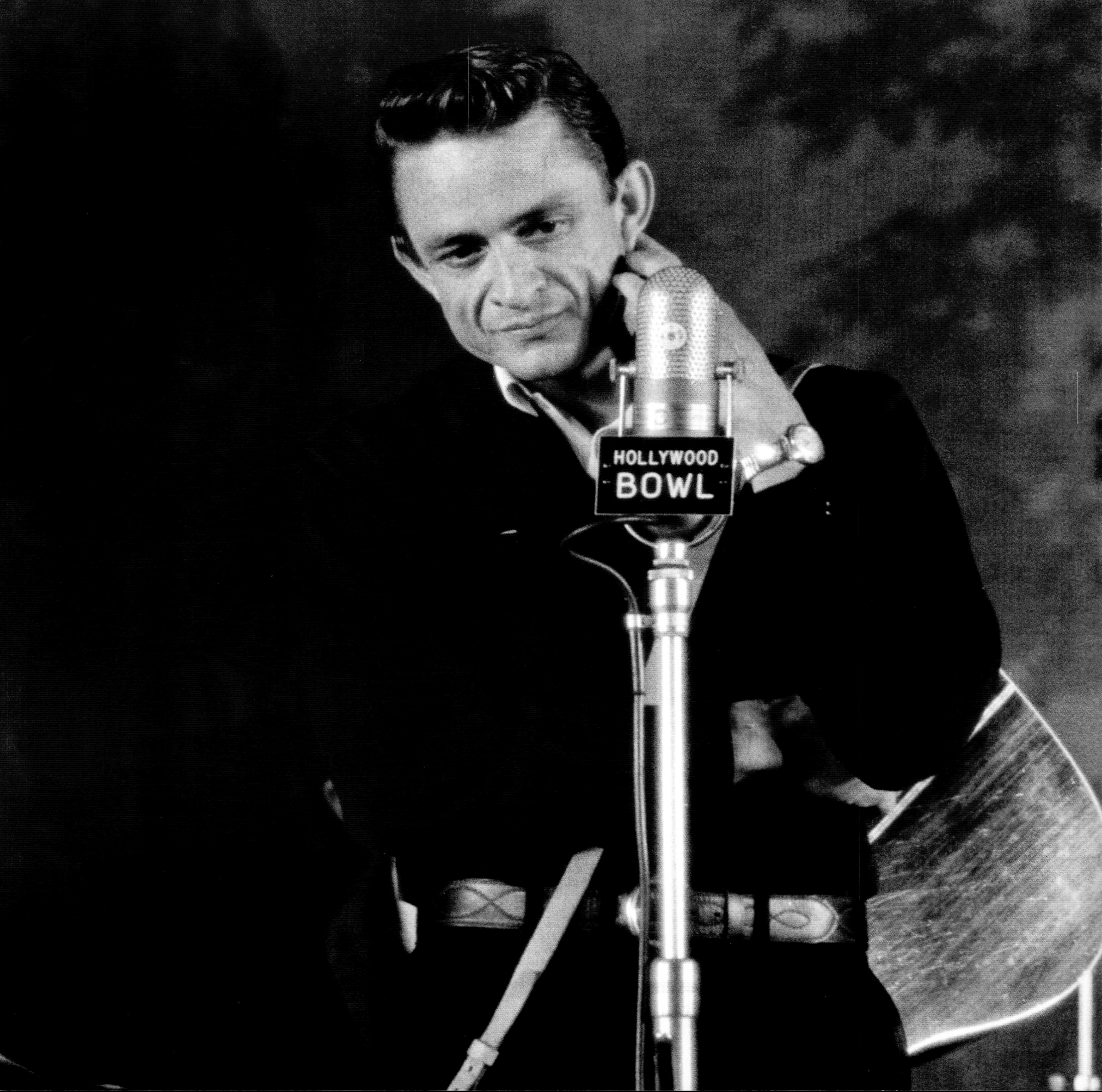
HOLLYWOOD
BOWL

interested and entertained. I was personable, outgoing, energetic—I loved everybody!

So the deception was complete, and I used them more and more, until the time came in 1959 or '60 when I had to have them.

Meanwhile, by November 1959, Bob Neal had had enough of California. Whether because of the slow headway he was making in establishing himself professionally on the West Coast, or because of dissatisfaction over his comanager status with Stew Carnall, Neal returned to Tennessee.

So Neal left, and in the end the business relationship between Carnall and Cash lasted only eighteen months more. In an interview with Christopher Wren for the book *Winners Got Scars Too*, Carnall admitted that the drug usage in the Cash camp influenced the deteriorating business relationship between the two men:

"He'd be up pacing and extremely nervous and would say things that would not make sense," Carnall said of Cash. "He changed from a person I enjoyed being with to a person who was brooding and moody when the pills got hold of him."

In much the same way that Carnall had become involved in the management of Johnny Cash after booking Cash on a concert tour, Canadian promoter Saul Holiff inherited the manager post in July 1961. Holiff made a name for himself by promoting a number of country and western concerts in the 1950s and 1960s, including Canadian appearances by Johnny Cash, and remained as Cash's manager into the 1970s.

While Johnny Cash's reputation for strong concert performances was growing among fans of country music, a second reputation was also growing around Cash and company—that of boisterous practical jokers. Marshall Grant had already demonstrated a fondness for explosives in the group's early concert sojourns, fashioning homemade bombs which, when detonated, became tour highlights for the road-weary musicians.

In the early 1960s, though, with the Tennessee Two expanded to Three with the addition of former Carl Perkins drummer W.S. "Fluke"

ABOVE: *Johnny Cash's unpretentious personality on stage won him legions of fans while signed to Columbia.* OPPOSITE: *Given the dizzying pace of his concert schedule, Johnny Cash may have found the sign on this microphone helpful in reminding him just which stage he was on for this 1962 show.*

ABOVE: *The Man in Black in a pensive publicity photo.* OPPOSITE: *Cash's expression reflects the pressure on a musician to continually try to top his latest chart success with each new recording session.*

Holland, the shenanigans increased exponentially. Whether rearranging hotel furniture, setting off explosions in rental cars, pouring water out of windows onto hotel guests, painting their hotel rooms in outlandish colors, or staging fake shootings and abductions in front of unsuspecting witnesses, the Cash entourage set standards of road misbehavior that rivaled any bad conduct of the generations of rock bands yet to come.

A more benevolent Cash tradition, however, also began during this period. On January 1, 1960, after spending New Year's Eve shuttling between three California concert appearances, Johnny Cash performed the first of a series of concerts for prisoners at San Quentin.

Johnny's appearance was also going through changes—he was moving more and more toward the imagery of the Man in Black, as he began to favor darker clothing over the flashier outfits that characterized his Sun years.

In late 1961, just after Holiff assumed the manager role, Johnny, Vivian and their children moved into a new home in Casitas Springs, California. Cash had become enamored of the Ventura County area, relating with the area's relatively wide open spaces. So taken was Johnny with the area next to the Pacific that he arranged for his parents to move to California as well.

Of course, part of the rationale for the Cash move to California in the first place had been to position Johnny Cash for a turn on the silver screen, and in autumn of 1960 Cash went before the cameras in the Flower Films production of *Five Minutes to Live*. Not remembered fondly when remembered at all, this film featured Johnny Cash in the role of a maniacal killer, and the ensemble cast included such luminaries as Vic Tayback, who would go on to pop culture fame and fortune on the television series *Alice* as Mel of Mel's Diner.

Though he may have been living in California and trying to break into the film business, throughout 1959 and 1960 Johnny Cash's recordings for Columbia were made back in Nashville at Owen Bradley's famed studio. This studio was where countless country stars like Patsy Cline and Patti Page had recorded their biggest hits, and Cash laid down many tracks with Bradley in the months immediately after his signing with Columbia.

After Cash's first two Columbia releases—the debut *The Fabulous Johnny Cash* and the religious album *Hymns by Johnny Cash*—came several sessions in March 1959 that resulted in *Songs of Our Soil.* This was the first album whose title reflected Cash's growing interest in presenting songs that portrayed America's heritage, good and bad.

With lucrative roadwork taking precedence over everything else, however, it's not surprising that studio sessions were often rushed affairs. The goal was to get product down on tape, and it was producer Don Law's job to keep things moving when Cash, Perkins, and Grant made a visit to the Bradley Film & Recording Studio.

With modern rock bands regularly taking months—if not years—to record a single release, it seems hard to believe that all songs but one on Johnny's fourth and fifth albums—the country record *Now There Was a Song* and the Americana of *Ride This Train*—were recorded in just three sessions. But that's exactly what happened between August 15 and 17, 1960, as Cash cut twenty-one songs in a total of about thirteen hours. For this studio date, Tennessee Three road drummer Fluke Holland was replaced by legendary session drummer Buddy Harman, who has provided rhythms for everyone from Patsy Cline to Jerry Lee Lewis during his career. Cash pal Johnny Western added some rhythm guitar, Floyd Cramer provided piano, and Gordon Terry fiddled during the fast-paced sessions.

Almost on cue, the first two singles from *Now There Was a Song,* "Seasons of My Heart" and "Honkey Tonk Girl" climbed the charts, reaching the upper echelon and solidifying Johnny Cash's reputation as a solid hitmaker. After lengthy tours of the United States and Europe, Cash's income for 1960 was now almost double that of the year before, and sales of his Columbia albums and singles didn't seem adversely affected by the albums that Sam Phillips had culled from the leftover Sun sessions material.

Cash's professional connection to Canada, initially established with the arrival of new manager Saul Holiff from Ontario, was duly enforced when Frank Jones began working on Cash recording sessions late in 1960. Don Law, the head of Columbia's country and western division and the man who had brought Johnny Cash to the label, was assigned Jones, who entered the record business in Canada, as an assistant, and the two men went on to oversee Cash's recordings throughout the 1960s.

ABOVE: *Cash favors a darkened atmosphere while recording at Columbia's Nashville studio on 16th Avenue South.* OPPOSITE: *In the early days the most basic of guitars did the job, but Cash's growing popularity allowed him to get this custom Gibson with his name emblazoned on the fretboard.*

June Carter was part of a respected country music family when Johnny Cash fell in love with her. Here June is shown kicking up her heels at the Grand Ole Opry (left) and posing with Mother Maybelle and the Carter Sisters (right).

Meanwhile, Holiff was rather cleverly turning the Johnny Cash concert tours into a self-contained touring package, with opening acts like Merle Travis and Johnny Western getting the crowd warmed up for the Man in Black. As the tour package grew, it brought even more well-known names aboard, including Carl Perkins and the Carter Family.

Possibly influencing the decision to bring the Carter Family into the show was Johnny's growing interest in June Carter, daughter of country music legend "Mother Maybelle" Carter. At home in California, Johnny's marriage with Vivian seemed to be disintegrating, probably because Cash was away on the road for such long periods of time. His

erratic behavior, caused by his dependence on pills, hastened the divorce that now seemed inevitable. In June 1966 Johnny Cash left his California home for a tour and never returned.

Not that June Carter was any more at ease with Cash's drug abuse than Vivian had been. When she would spy Johnny attempting to get pills or a prescription to obtain them from a doctor paying a backstage visit, she would do her best to intercede. But when someone feels that they need drugs to get by, the good intentions of loved ones to stop the supply often stand no chance against the user's sheer determination. And Johnny Cash has often admitted that he was a determined user.

THE JOHNNY CASH SOUND

The second you hear it, you know who it is. The Johnny Cash sound is one of the most recognizable of any recording artist in the world. But what makes that sound so unique?

For most of Johnny Cash's early career, much of the credit goes to Luther Perkins, who was the Tennessee Three's guitar player from the time they were the Tennessee Two until his death in 1968. Speculation is that Luther's wide-open-spaces style came as a result of the guitarist's fear of making mistakes, hence his halting, carefully chosen selection of notes that graced each immaculate solo. Whether that's true or not, Sam Phillips recognized Luther's style as being something out of the ordinary from the moment he heard it and was encouraged to sign Cash.

But at the heart of the Johnny Cash rhythm is the sound that's come to be known as "boom-chicka boom-chicka." In its simplest format, it consists of a bass note on guitar immediately followed by a strum down across higher strings then a strum back up. That's followed by an alternating bass note and again the strum down and back up. Speed up the process just described and you get the "riding the rails" sound that has characterized so much of Johnny Cash's music.

"It doesn't matter to me that I only know three or four chords," Cash has said of his rhythm work. "With the left fingers on the frets, the heel of my right hand hugging the body of the guitar, letting just my right thumb lead and drive the rhythm, sometimes it's magic, and I just believe that when it all comes together it's the right way for me to do it."

The traditional propulsion of the boom-chicka lick—also known as the Carter Family scratch for their reliance on the same style—has been used by countless artists, some having explored its use long before Johnny Cash played his first notes. But it's probably safe to say that none have refined its use to the degree perfected by Johnny Cash and the Tennessee Three.

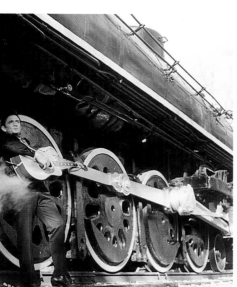

The rhythmic undertow of many of Johnny Cash's hits call to mind the sound of the railroad, a sound that symbolized a nation on the move.

But things were progressing on the creative front. While Cash had suffered a string of disappointing performances from his singles released in 1961 and 1962, all that suddenly changed in mid-1963 with the release of "Ring of Fire." Written by June Carter and Merle Kilgore, who were both now part of the traveling Johnny Cash show, "Love's Ring of Fire" (as it was originally called) was first recorded by June's sister Anita. Cash liked the song, and vowed that if it wasn't a hit for Anita Carter he would give it a shot himself.

When Cash prepared to record the song in March 1963, he told Don Law that he had had a dream in which "Love's Ring of Fire" was enhanced by, of all things, a mariachi horn arrangement. Law and Frank Jones, producers of many of Cash's greatest hits, went along with the idea. Recorded on March 25, with the title shortened to "Ring of Fire," the song was released by Columbia on April 19. By July it was solidly entrenched in the number one spot on the country charts and had hit number seventeen on the pop charts as well.

In March 1964 Cash entered the Columbia Studios in Nashville to update some of his biggest hits from the Sun Records days, as well as to work through some new material. One of the new tunes to come out of those sessions, "Understand Your Man," climbed to the top of the charts.

Despite all his commercial success during this era, Johnny Cash should also be recognized for his exploration of thematic albums. While "rock operas" became a much-ballyhooed form throughout the late 1960s and into the 1970s, Johnny Cash had already released several albums that covered a central theme. And, as evidenced by the liner notes he penned for *Mean As Hell! Ballads from the True West*, Johnny Cash took his research for these recordings seriously.

How did I get ready for this album? I followed trails in my Jeep and on foot, and I slept under mesquite bushes and in gullies. I heard the timber wolves, looked for golden nuggets in old creek beds, sat for hours beneath a manzanita bush in an ancient

Indian burial ground, breathed the west wind and heard the tales it tells only to those who listen. I replaced a wooden grave marker of some man in the Arizona who "never made it." I walked across alkali flats where others had walked before me, but hadn't made it. I ate mesquite beans and squeezed the water from a barrel cactus. I was saved once by a forest ranger, lying flat on my face, starving. I learned to throw a Bowie knife and kill a jack rabbit at forty yards, not for the sport but because I was hungry. I learned of the true West the hard way—a la 1965.

Indeed, some of Johnny Cash's most inspired performances were found in the grooves of these records. "Mean As Hell," with its spoken introduction telling the tale of how the West got so tough, and "25 Minutes to Go," the harrowing recitation of a doomed man watching the minutes pass leading to his death, are nothing but convincing thanks to Cash's gut-level presentation. But the storytelling and interpretive genius of Johnny Cash was being threatened by the very lifestyle that made many of his recorded performances so riveting.

In *Man in Black*, he recounts how he suffered through the darkest days of his drug dependence: "The furies literally clawed at my brain. Every move of every muscle was torture from the days and nights of abuse. My nerves were at a screaming breaking point." The drugs, alcohol, and cigarettes were robbing Johnny Cash—and his audience—of his wonderful voice. Cash could barely croak his way through a prestigious performance at New York's Carnegie Hall, and his vocal troubles were becoming so acute that his performances on stage or in the studio could not be relied on.

Still, as Cash wrote in his autobiography, no matter how low he had sunk or how many foolish risks he took, he maintained his faith that God was looking after him.

I know that the hand of God was never off me, no matter what condition I was in, for there is no other way to explain my escaping the many, many accidents I had. Besides wrecking every car I had for seven years, I totaled two Jeeps and a camper and turned over two tractors and a bulldozer. I sank two boats in

separate accidents on a lake, and I jumped from a truck just before it went over a six-hundred-foot [182.9m] cliff in California.

In 1965 Johnny Cash made a guest appearance at the Grand Ole Opry after a long stint of pill usage. When he walked on the stage of the Ryman Auditorium and stepped up to the microphone, he was unable to remove the microphone from the stand that held it. In a sudden fit of rage he hurled the stand down, then hauled it across the floor, shattering many of the footlights across the Ryman stage. The glass littered the floor and fell into the audience.

The band stopped playing and Cash left the stage. He came face to face with the manager of the Grand Ole Opry, who had only one thing to say:

"We can't use you on the Opry any more, John."

Johnny Cash, looking the part on the cover of his Mean As Hell *album.*

Note Marshall Grant's standup bass getting a boost from the large amplifier resting on its side, during a Johnny Cash appearance at the Grand Ole Opry. Grant eventually switched to the more compact electric bass.

CHAPTER 5

FALL
FROM GRACE

Although the personal

fortunes of Johnny Cash were

taking a dire turn for the worse

in the early 1960s, his professional

fortunes were headed in quite the opposite

direction—Johnny Cash was well on the

road to superstardom. Interestingly, at a stage

when most artists close ranks and stick with

what they know, Cash was exploring new ideas.

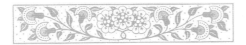

ABOVE: *Cash looks a little weary after a decade's worth of concert appearances.* PAGES 56–57: *June Carter, Johnny Cash, and Carl Perkins take a turn at the microphone at the 1969 Newport Folk Festival in Rhode Island.*

In 1964 Cash had appeared at the famed Newport Folk Festival, cementing a connection with followers of folk music that was beneficial to him from both an artistic and financial standpoint. Where pop music fans tended to flit from hit to hit, following whatever single happened to be hot on the radio, the folk fans were a more pensive lot. They preferred to listen to whole albums as they explored the feelings conveyed in an album's worth of protests or revelations. For Johnny Cash, who had already been working with the idea of unified concept recordings, this album-oriented audience that was now accepting his music was a godsend.

The turning point that raised Cash's stock with the folk crowd—and alarmed the country music chart watchers—came with the controversy surrounding the release of the single "The Ballad of Ira Hayes."

Ira Hayes was a Pima Indian immortalized in one of the greatest images of America's history—the raising of the flag above Iwo Jima in World War II. But despite his inclusion in the glorious moment, he returned home from war to a tragic life of poverty and alcoholism. Songwriter Peter LaFarge—himself a full-blooded Nargaset Indian who was raised by Hopi Indians—further immortalized Hayes in a grim, true-life ballad.

Cash, having become fascinated with the folk world after visiting New York's Greenwich Village and meeting and hearing musicians like Bob Dylan, decided that he not only would record "The Ballad of Ira Hayes," but would create an entire album of songs about the Indian. The result was *Bitter Tears*, one of Cash's strongest recordings.

While the folk world embraced both *Bitter Tears* and Cash's performance at Newport, in the summer of 1964 the country music disc jockeys were decidedly uncomfortable with "The Ballad of Ira Hayes" and this new direction Johnny's music was taking.

Johnny Cash was never one to shy away from saying what was on his mind and, in a full-page ad in the August 22 issue of *Billboard* magazine, the music industry bible, Cash lambasted a country music establishment that was reluctant to accept his songs of bitter reality. Above the apt Columbia Records tag line "Nobody but nobody more original than Johnny Cash," Cash wrote in part:

DJs—station managers—owners, etc., where are your guts?

I'm not afraid to sing the hard, bitter lines that the son of Oliver LaFarge wrote…

Classify me, categorize me—STIFLE me, but it won't work…

I am fighting no particular cause. If I did, it would soon make me a sluggard. For as time changes, I change.

You're right! Teenage girls and Beatle-record buyers don't want to hear this sad story of Ira Hayes—but who cries more easily, and who always go to sad movies to cry??? Teenage girls.

Some of you "Top Forty" DJs went all out for this at first. Thanks anyway. Maybe the program director or station manager will reconsider.

This ad (go ahead and call it that) costs like hell. Would you, or those pulling the strings for you, go to the mike with a new approach? That is, listen again to the record?

Regardless of the trade charts—the categorizing, classifying and restrictions of air play, this is not a country song, not as it is being sold. It is a fine reason though for the gutless to give it thumbs down.

"Ballad of Ira Hayes" is strong medicine. So is Rochester—Harlem—Birmingham and Vietnam…

I've blown my horn now, just this once, then no more. Since I've said these things now, I find myself not caring if the record is programmed or not. I won't ask you to cram it down their throats.

But… I had to fight back when I realized that so many stations are afraid of "Ira Hayes."

Just one question: WHY???

Not surprisingly, this unprecedented and vitriolic public attack aimed at the staid country music broadcasting establishment was not very well received. Reactions ranged from continued indifference to Cash's new song to demands that Cash be stripped of his membership in the Country Music Association. As one editor of a country music magazine indignantly stated in print, "you and your crowd are just too intelligent to associate with plain country folks, country artists, and country DJs."

Johnny Cash onstage with his longtime drummer, W. S. Holland.

Nor did the tempest blow "The Ballad of Ira Hayes" to the top of the charts. While the single edged its way fitfully up the country charts, it didn't even register on the pop charts. And when the album *Bitter Tears*—a recording that Cash has referred to as one of his best works—was released in October, *Billboard* did not even review it. Despite all the controversy and *Billboard's* spurning of the record, *Bitter Tears* still sold more than 100 thousand copies—an indication of the commercial strength Cash still wielded and the loyalty of his fans.

Just as the brouhaha over "Ira Hayes" was about to break, Johnny Cash signed a new vocal quartet into his touring organization: The Statler Brothers. Originally a traditional gospel quartet operating under the name The Kingsmen, they appropriated a

new name thanks to the regional Statler Paper Company and proceeded to build popularity with a show that mixed their original gospel with pop and country material.

The Statler Brothers stayed with the touring Johnny Cash show into the mid-1970s, and Cash used his influence to get them a recording contract with Columbia soon after they signed on with him. Clearly, a professional relationship with Johnny Cash was a smart career move for up-and-coming talent.

Being arrested, however, was not a smart move—and that's just what happened to Johnny Cash on October 2, 1965.

At this time, Cash was still heavily dependent on pills to get through the grind of the endless touring. That dependence found him crossing the border from Juarez, Mexico, into El Paso, Texas, carrying hundreds of pills that he had been able to purchase thanks to a "helpful" cab driver.

Cash was generally able to obtain his pill supply legally from doctors, and it's important to remember that this was a time in America

when many people thought it was perfectly normal to take strong drugs for any number of reasons. Indeed, it was often truck drivers relying on pills to make it through long hauls on the interstates who turned road-weary country musicians onto the "benefits" of speed pills. But on this occasion, Cash made the unfortunate decision to obtain his pills outside legal channels.

Before flying out of El Paso that night, Cash hid most of the drugs inside a guitar and boarded his flight. But before the plane bound for Los Angeles could take off, police boarded the aircraft and escorted Johnny from the plane. He had been observed crossing the border back into the United States, and the authorities felt they had enough justification to prevent Cash from leaving town while they searched his possessions. Their suspicions of illegal activities were soon confirmed.

Although the authorities had hoped to make a heroin arrest—the cab driver obtained Cash's pills from a known heroin dealer—they

ABOVE: *Cash clowns around with his good friend and partner in music, Carl Perkins.*   OPPOSITE: *The Johnny Cash show in full force before the people of San Antonio, Texas, with Cash's vocals augmented by the Carters to the left and the Statler Brothers on the right.*

COHORTS AND COSTARS

It is often said that a man can be measured by the company he keeps. If that's true, Johnny Cash certainly meets the standards of an American music legend.

Over the years Cash has recorded in literally hundreds of studio sessions with hundreds of musicians. Among those are the Tennessee Three—Marshall Grant on bass, W.S. Holland on drums, and Luther Perkins and later Bob Wootton on guitar—the Carter Family, and the Statler Brothers. And let's not forget Carl Perkins, who often added his guitar wizardry to Cash sessions. But there was also Marty Stuart, a brilliant young musician who joined Johnny Cash on guitar in 1979 and has gone on to become one of today's brightest country music stars. And then there's Johnny's associates in the Highwayman quartet: Willie Nelson, Waylon Jennings, and Kris Kristofferson.

But besides all the studio session aces who have joined the collaborators mentioned above, there is a whole galaxy of stars who have sought out and recorded with Johnny Cash in the hopes of adding to the legend. Here is a list of just some of the musicians—from all styles of music—who have contributed to the Johnny Cash studio legacy: Merle Haggard, Paul and Linda McCartney, Bob Dylan, U2 and Brian Eno, Tom Petty, Flea (of the Red Hot Chili Peppers), Mick Fleetwood (of Fleetwood Mac), Ernest Tubb, Jerry Lee Lewis, Boots Randolph, Rita Coolidge, David Allen Coe, Joan Baez, Billy Gibbons (of ZZ Top), New Riders of the Purple Sage, Ricky Skaggs, Emmylou Harris, Oscar the Grouch, Nick Lowe, Julie Andrews, Levon Helm (of The Band), Bill Monroe, Hoyt Axton, James Burton, Travis Tritt, Dave Edmunds, John Fogerty, Rick Nelson, Roy Orbison, Glen Danzig, The Judds, Roy Acuff, Don and Phil Everly, Glen Campbell, Charlie Daniels, Nitty Gritty Dirt Band, the Jordanaires, Tom T. Hall, and George Jones.

And the list grows rapidly with each passing year.

PAGE 62, TOP LEFT: *Johnny Cash with the Highwaymen, Willie Nelson, Kris Kristofferson, and Waylon Jennings (left to right).* **TOP RIGHT:** *Cash laughs as Bob Dylan lays low.* **BOTTOM:** *Early in his career Cash was thrilled to be performing with the legendary Ernest Tubb.*

PAGE 63, ABOVE: *Cash shares a laugh with another American institution, the great Louis Armstrong.* **LEFT:** *Johnny smiles in admiration of the picking ability of Roy Clark.*

decided to press charges anyway, since the pill supply had been obtained illegally. Johnny Cash spent the night in jail, and was photographed in handcuffs as he was led from his cell to the courthouse to post bail the next morning.

But the arrest itself wasn't the only insulting incident associated with Cash's sojourn south of the border. Despite their worsening relationship, his wife, Vivian, came to be with Johnny in the wake of his arrest. The two were photographed leaving the courthouse together. The National States Rights Party—a militant group whose views paralleled those of the Ku Klux Klan—saw the photographs and somehow arrived at the conclusion that Mrs. Cash's skin shade was just a bit too dark. "Arrest Exposes Johnny Cash's Negro Wife" read an unpleasant leaflet distributed by the group, complete with one of the allegedly offensive photos. They also set up a recorded telephone announcement designed to expose Cash and his family to the world. But despite a few Ku Klux Klan protests at Cash shows immediately after the arrest, manager Saul Holiff did an admirable job of damage control with the racial allegations and the Klan's harassment.

Later, when Cash's trial took place in El Paso, he received what amounted to a slap on the wrist. Cash was fined one thousand dollars and given a thirty-day suspended sentence.

Johnny's relationship with Vivian, however, did not survive his latest troubling incident, despite her public support of him during this time—the numerous problems and never-ending strain of Cash's life on the road had destroyed the marriage. Cash moved his base of operations from California to Nashville, while Vivian remained on the West Coast and established a successful chain of beauty parlors.

Once back in Tennessee, the rootless Cash at first stayed with Ezra and Maybelle Carter or bunked at producer Don Law's apartment. For a time, Johnny even had a place that he shared with a singer-songwriter newly arrived on Music Row from Phoenix, Arizona—Waylon Jennings. But eventually Cash purchased his own home after spying an appealing house under construction while out and about Nashville with Waylon one day.

While recording in Nashville, Cash met a young man who was trying to earn a living working in Columbia's studio doing odd jobs while

This photograph of Johnny Cash was distributed by the Associated Press accompanying the news of Cash's October 1965 arrest in El Paso, Texas.

Kris Kristofferson first met Johnny Cash shortly after Kristofferson arrived in Nashville and was employed doing odd jobs at Columbia's studio. Years later Kristofferson, a successful singer/songwriter himself, appeared on Cash's television show.

the young Tennessean was even booked by Ed Sullivan to perform his hit on national television in early 1956. But it was not to be.

Tragedy struck after a show in Norfolk, Virginia, as Perkins' group headed north toward New York. Their rented limousine ran off the road near Dover, Delaware. Carl woke three days later with numerous broken bones, lacerations, and a fractured skull. His brother, Jay, eventually died from injuries sustained in the crash. The mounting progress that Carl Perkins had made toward stardom came to a grinding halt.

Although Perkins struggled mightily to regain his musical stature—and was helped in his efforts by the attentions of a new British band known as The Beatles—he was unable to regain the momentum that his career had once had.

In late 1965 Perkins injured his leg with a shotgun in a hunting accident. So when Johnny Cash visited him in January, and asked if Perkins would like to join his show, the rockabilly master was quick to take Johnny up on his offer.

ABOVE: *Loretta Lynn and the Man in Black face a list of questions from interviewer David Frost during a Country Music Association presentation.* OPPOSITE: *Cash cemented his reputation with countless live appearances.*

waiting for his songwriting talents to be discovered: Kris Kristofferson. Cash struck up a friendship with Kristofferson, and began helpfully spreading the word about the young man's abilities.

During this time, Cash was making new friends such as Waylon and Kris, but he never forgot his old pals. In fact, one of Johnny's oldest musician friends—Carl Perkins—became part of the Cash show in 1966. Perkins was the same age as Johnny, and they shared the common heritage of having launched their careers at Sun Records. Perkins had seemed to be on a trajectory toward stardom—after all, his "Blue Suede Shoes" had been a huge hit both for him and for Elvis Presley. Perkins' version alone had racked up sales of more than two million copies, and

ABOVE: *A Sioux chief presents Cash with regalia during a concert at Rosebud Reservation in South Dakota. Cash has often demonstrated a profound interest in the affairs of Native Americans.*

Carter Family recorded songs that made up the uncharacteristic album *Everybody Loves a Nut.*

This new and atypical album climbed to the top five on the country charts in July based on the strength of songs like "Dirty Old Egg Sucking Dog" and "The Bug That Tried to Crawl Around the World." And who knows how far up the charts the album may have climbed had it included the colorfully-titled "Flushed From the Bathroom of Your Heart," which had been recorded for *Everybody Loves a Nut* but was eventually left in the archives?

While *Everybody Loves a Nut* was a funny album, life on the road was no laughing matter. Johnny Cash's condition was deteriorating, with missed shows being the result. June Carter, Carl Perkins, and the others in the show would gamely try to fill in, but it was Johnny Cash who the audiences had paid to see.

Throughout 1966 and 1967, Cash tried again and again to quit taking pills, and again and again his dependence overcame his resolve. June Carter and Marshall Grant did their best to help Johnny, but to no avail.

Finally, in November 1967, Johnny Cash came to a crossroads, when he was jailed in Lafayette, Georgia, after he was spotted wandering around suspiciously. Cash was booked for drunkenness and was sent to a cell by Sheriff Ralph Jones to sober up. Jones also confiscated Cash's pill supply upon booking the singer.

Jones and his wife were tremendous fans of Cash, and the next morning, rather than press charges, the sheriff decided to let Johnny go. But before Cash left, Sheriff Jones called him aside. He told Johnny how important Cash's music was to him and his wife and how upsetting it had been for Jones to see Cash in such a bedraggled and sad state. Speaking man to man, Jones challenged Cash to straighten his life out.

Days later, Johnny Cash made a true and determined effort to do just that.

Meanwhile, early 1966 was consumed with an attempt at recording a lighthearted collection of songs that would stand in direct contrast with Johnny Cash's somber image. Producers Don Law and Frank Jones oversaw the sessions, in which Cash, the Tennessee Three, and the

ABOVE: *Johnny Cash had settled into a look that exuded dignified confidence in this 1970 photo.* RIGHT: *Sheriff Ralph Jones (far right) looks on with pride as Johnny Cash performs in 1970. Sheriff Jones had arrested Cash in Lafayette, Georgia, in 1967 and challenged him to take charge of his life.*

CHAPTER 6

FACING
THE MUSIC

A depiction of Johnny Cash's

withdrawal from drugs,

as he described it in *Man In Black*:

"Sometimes in addition to glass

coming out of my skin and the corners of my

eyes, I would be pulling splinters of wood and bri-

ars and thorns out of my flesh, and sometimes worms.

I wanted to scream but I couldn't.

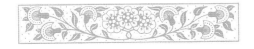

Withdrawal. It's a heavy drug user's worst nightmare. And once it has been suffered through, a return to drug dependence is almost guaranteed unless the user is absolutely determined to quit. But after that night in a Georgia jail late in 1967, Johnny Cash felt that determination to quit. Mother Maybelle and June Carter went to see Dr. Nat Winston, a psychiatrist who was serving as Tennessee's State Commissioner of Mental Health, to see if he could help them and Johnny deal with Johnny's problem. Winston was friends with many of country music's biggest stars and, although he was at first reluctant to take on the challenge, Mother Maybelle and June convinced him to help Johnny Cash conquer his dependence on pills.

"You can't believe how tense he was when he was on pills," Winston told Christopher Wren during an interview for *Winners Got Scars Too.* "He was haggard, a mess. He was out of control. I don't think he would have lived much longer. He would have died or killed himself in an accident. In some ways, he enjoyed the pathos. He knew he had great talent and was burning himself out. But I never sensed any suicidal tendencies in John. He wants to live forever."

To do that, though, Cash had to give up the pills. He got the final shove to do so just days after that night in the Georgia jail.

Having succumbed to the lure of his pills once again, Cash had nearly driven a tractor into a lake near his house. Exhausted from the

pills and soaking wet, Cash was unable to muster the strength to reach the warmth of his house on this freezing cold night. Fortunately his friend Braxton Dixon discovered him. June Carter arrived soon after, and at that moment Cash made the crucial decision—he had to get off the drugs. Nat Winston was summoned.

Winston had determined that the only way to get Cash fully withdrawn was to basically imprison him in his own house. Aiding Winston would be June Carter, Carl Perkins, W.S. Holland, and others with Cash's best interests at heart. They not only would have to look after Cash but would be required to chase away pill dealers and others whose presence might have had a detrimental effect on Johnny's successful withdrawal.

The rest, however, was up to Johnny Cash. He had only his will and his faith in God to help him through the suffering—and suffer he did. The pains of his withdrawal—particularly the physical dependency he had developed for tranquilizers—tore at his mind and body. But with the help of daily visits from Nat Winston and the presence of those closest to him—especially June Carter—Cash began to conquer his dependency. He began to put on weight, regaining his appetite and filling out his frame. But the real test was yet to come.

Just three weeks after beginning his withdrawal, Johnny Cash was back out on the road, following a benefit performance for Hendersonville High School, near his home. June and the others must

ABOVE: *Johnny Cash at Folsom Prison, his expression reflecting the atmosphere of the grim site.* OPPOSITE: *June and Johnny walk through the gates at Kansas State Prison as a guard watches from the tower.* PAGES 70–71: *June Carter Cash sings as Johnny Cash and the Tennessee Three, augmented by Carl Perkins (second from right), provide musical accompaniment.*

have known that, had he really wanted them, Cash could have obtained more pills and started the vicious cycle all over again. But he didn't. He remained clear of the danger, and the rave reviews his concerts were receiving pointed to a new enthusiasm for his craft.

In fact, Johnny Cash even began to work to help Carl Perkins conquer his problems with alcohol. Where once the two had reinforced each other's worst impulses and misbehavior, now they helped each other cope with sobriety on the road.

As 1968 dawned on a revitalized Johnny Cash, he played a triumphant live performance with the Tennessee Three, the Carter Family, and the Statler Brothers at Folsom Prison in California. The show was recorded for a live album, and when it was released in the summer, *Johnny Cash At Folsom Prison* rocketed to number one on the country charts and cracked the top fifteen on the pop charts.

At the same time, Johnny Cash began a policy of playing make-up performances, making amends for shows he had missed when the drugs had held sway over his behavior. This move only served to earn Cash greater respect in the music world.

As gratifying as his continued professional success must have been, however, perhaps the most important moment of Johnny Cash's life came with his marriage to June Carter.

Cash's divorce from Vivian—filed for by his wife a year and a half before—became final on January 3, 1968. June herself had been through two marriages that had ended in divorce. But after all they had been through, it was clear that Johnny and June were very much in love.

In February 1968 Johnny and June were onstage in London, Ontario, in front of five thousand people when Cash proposed. Much to the pleasure of the audience, June accepted.

Nashville got wind of the wedding plans during an awards show on February 29. Johnny Cash accepted an award with the comment, "This will be a fine wedding present."

The next day, March 1, 1968, June Carter and Johnny Cash were wed in a small ceremony in Franklin, Kentucky. A festive reception took place that night at Cash's Hendersonville home and was attended by country music stars like Roger Miller and Webb Pierce.

With Johnny Cash now married, and with his physical and mental condition much improved, a long and troubled chapter in his career seemed to close. Cash himself admitted as much to Christopher Wren at the time:

"Most everybody had written me off. Oh yeah, they all acted like they were proud for me when I straightened up. Some of them are still

ABOVE: *Johnny and his wife, June Carter, posed for this publicity photo in 1971.* OPPOSITE: *June and Johnny's enduring relationship has helped the Man in Black through some of the darkest times in his life.*

ABOVE: *Johnny Cash plays San Quentin. The follow-up to the Folsom Prison show was even more successful than its predecessor.* OPPOSITE: *Before an audience of eight hundred former convicts, Cash performs to benefit Georgia's early release program.*

IN THE JAILHOUSE

Two of the biggest selling albums of the 1960s were Johnny Cash's live recordings at California's Folsom Prison in 1968 and at San Quentin Prison in 1969.

For Cash, however, the prison recordings were not just a clever marketing tool or something done just to get attention. Cash had logged many hours performing free of charge for prisoners, and had offered his first concert at San Quentin back in 1960—nearly a decade before these two live recordings were committed to tape.

Columbia's Don Law had agreed with Cash's desire to do a live prison recording, even though others at Columbia were less enthusiastic about the idea. And although Law had been forced into retirement before the idea came to fruition at Folsom in 1968—Columbia's Bob Johnston eventually oversaw the live recording—the value of the plan was proven as *Johnny Cash At Folsom Prison* quickly racked up sales of more than two million copies. Cash sounded even more confident in his performance on *Johnny Cash At San Quentin*, and this second recording even surpassed its predecessor in sales.

Despite the commercial success, however, Johnny Cash never forgot the men behind bars, and he continued to perform a number of concerts at prisons throughout the country.

Both of the Columbia prison recordings were fine documentations of a wildly enthusiastic audience cheering on Johnny Cash as he performed a great selection of material running the gamut from harrowing to hysterically funny. As is often the case with live recordings, however, a substantial amount of the material performed on those two days remains in the vaults. The issued recordings presented highlights of the concerts, edited and with the occasional obscenity bleeped out. Remaining unheard are moments like the performance at Folsom of Marshall Grant's "Long-Legged Guitar Pickin' Man" and multiple takes of "Folsom Prison Blues" recorded at San Quentin.

Johnny Cash fans can only hope that some day the full recordings of the Folsom and San Quentin shows will be issued in unedited form. Such a release would stand as a fascinating testament to the special relationship between the Man in Black and the men behind bars.

mad about it, though. I didn't go ahead and die so they'd have a legend to sing about and put me in hillbilly heaven!"

Now, though, June and Johnny began to show a greater interest in learning and studying both their own faith and the religions of others. This fascination led to their first trip to Israel (following a European tour in June), where the two visited sacred places and soaked in the history that surrounded them.

Unfortunately, on August 3, 1968, the happiness that Johnny Cash must have felt over his marriage to June and the results of his battle against the pills was suddenly tempered by tragedy. Before dawn, Cash received a devastating telephone call from Luther Perkins' wife. Luther was in the hospital, gravely burned after falling asleep in his living room with a lit cigarette in his hand. The guitarist—one of the most distinctive players in the history of country music—died two days later, having never regained consciousness.

Luther's death was a shocking blow. The guitarist had been at Cash's side every step of the journey to stardom, and his playing style was a crucial element in the sound of Johnny Cash. For all of August and most of September, Carl Perkins did his best to fill Luther's shoes as a temporary member of the Tennessee Three, but Cash, Marshall Grant, and W.S. Holland were uncertain what to do about a full-time guitarist.

The answer walked backstage on September 17, 1968, in Fayetteville, Arkansas. Johnny and W.S. were awaiting the arrival of Marshall and Carl for the evening's performance, but they never made it. The two flights out of Memphis that Marshall and Carl attempted to make were canceled due to bad weather; a third flight suffered mechanical failure just prior to takeoff. By the time Marshall and Carl finally got airborne in a small chartered jet, Johnny Cash and W.S. Holland were already on stage. And joining them on guitar was a young man named Bob Wootton.

Bob Wootton had been born in Arkansas and had moved to California, where he had taken up the guitar at the age of eleven. Like Johnny, Wootton had honed his musical instincts during a stint in the armed forces (in his case, the army). And Wootton had learned and

ABOVE: *Johnny has always had a strong, commanding presence onstage.* OPPOSITE: *With his lasting stardom assured, Cash often took advantage of the chance to sing gospel music—a desire discouraged by those who oversaw his early career.*

ABOVE: *Johnny Cash sings in Sweden, at Stockholm's Philadelphia Church in 1972. At this appearance Cash spoke of having found peace through Jesus, and of his battle with drug use.*   RIGHT: *In 1970 at the Knoxville, Tennessee, Billy Graham Crusade, Johnny Cash sings praises backed by Marshall Grant (partially obscured at left), W.S. Holland (center), and Carl Perkins (right).*

ABOVE: *"The Johnny Cash of Japan," Takahiro Saito (center), meets the real thing and Eddy Arnold (left) during a taping for the television special "Johnny Cash Presents the Country Music Story."* LEFT: *"Mother Maybelle" Carter accompanies her son-in-law on an NBC television special in 1974.*

studied the songs of his country music idols, just as Johnny had. But for Wootton one musician in particular exerted the greatest influence—Johnny Cash.

On that warm September evening, Bob Wootton drove down from his home in Tulsa, where he had settled after leaving the army, in the hopes of meeting Johnny Cash at the show in Fayetteville. And when he did meet Cash that night, he found a country music star with no guitarist or bass player for the show at hand. When Wootton offered his services as a guitar player for the evening, Cash readily accepted.

The years of playing Cash's material paid off. The show went well, and even though Johnny told Bob that he wasn't looking for a new guitar player, he did take Wootton's phone number.

Two days later, Bob Wootton received a phone call from Johnny Cash to come play in Harrison, Arkansas. Cash had talked things over with Holland, Grant, and Perkins. Johnny, June, and W.S. had all been impressed by Wootton's abilities that night in Fayetteville. The Harrison gig would give Marshall and Carl a chance to check out the guitarist.

In the end, Cash and company agreed: Wootton was definitely the man to fill Luther's shoes. And ever since that night in 1968, Bob Wootton has been Johnny Cash's guitarist and a member of the fabled Tennessee Three. In 1974, he also became a member of the family— when he married June's sister Anita.

By the end of 1968 Johnny Cash had earned two million dollars that year alone, a tremendous jump over the six hundred thousand dollars he had made in 1967. Clearly, Cash's new outlook was helping his career—but 1969 was to be even bigger.

The year began with Johnny and June traveling to the Far East, playing a tour that included numerous dates in Vietnam for the American servicemen. In the sweltering summer weather, Cash briefly fell back under the spell of drugs when he was taken sick early in the tour of hot, smoky clubs and ballrooms. Given pills by a hotel doctor in Manila, Cash briefly returned to the days of years gone by before recoiling from the dangers that the pills presented.

Just days after Cash returned to United States soil, he taped yet another live record at a prison. This time it was the notorious San Quentin prison in California on February 24.

When *Johnny Cash At San Quentin* was released in the summer, it climbed to the top of the country charts, just as *Johnny Cash At Folsom Prison* had. That probably wasn't too surprising, but what was a very pleasant surprise was that for the first time a Johnny Cash album went to number one on the pop charts as well. *San Quentin* sat in the number one pop position for four straight weeks, holding off competition from contemporary rock artists like The Beatles, Led Zeppelin, Cream, Creedence Clearwater Revival, and Jimi Hendrix.

The lead single from *At San Quentin* did nearly as well. The song— penned by children's writer Shel Silverstein, who had written various other Cash songs, such as "25 Minutes to Go"—was an unlikely tune called "A Boy Named Sue."

This song detailed the aggravation suffered by a boy given a girl's name. Cash had barely learned the song before recording it live in front

By 1970 Johnny Cash had reason to look beatific. With a successful television show and numerous hit singles, he was one of country's most popular stars.

of the inmates—while referring to sheets containing the song's lyrics, no less—but the spirit of the song and the raucous enthusiasm of the captive audience struck a nerve with the listening public. The result: number one on the country single charts, number two on the pop single charts.

As the Cash single "Daddy Sang Bass" had already visited the top of the charts earlier in the year, it was clear to the entire entertainment industry just how big a star Johnny Cash was. It was especially clear to the president of Columbia Records, Clive Davis. In his autobiography, *Clive: Inside the Record Business,* Davis recalled just how important Cash was to Columbia's fortunes:

"Johnny Cash had sold a staggering six and a half million albums in 1969, more albums than any individual artist had ever sold in one year."

Helping cement that popularity was *The Johnny Cash Show,* a weekly ABC television program that aired from June 7, 1969, into 1971. Almost the antithesis of a flashy Hollywood production, Cash's show was taped at venues like Nashville's hallowed Ryman Auditorium and stressed content over glitz. In fact, it was canceled only when Cash grew dissatisfied with pressures to move the program in the direction of a more typical variety show.

Guests on *The Johnny Cash Show* included such artists as Chet Atkins, Charley Pride, Ray Charles, Roy Orbison, Merle Haggard, Burl Ives, and—in an extremely rare network television appearance—Cash's friend Bob Dylan. Each of the shows also featured a segment called "Ride This Train," where Johnny would make the most of his opportunity to sing songs about the heritage and history of the United States.

Columbia's Clive Davis was amazed by Johnny Cash during the Country Music Weeks of the late 1960s and early 1970s. Sponsored by the Grand Ole Opry, Country Music Week allowed fans to flock into Nashville and see many of the greatest country stars. It was also a rendezvous for record label executives like Davis and other music industry personnel.

When Cash played during Country Music Week, Columbia and Davis would rent the Municipal Theatre for the free concert. And

OPPOSITE: *Performing with Ray Charles, Johnny Cash smiles as Charles performs one of his country crossover hits. Charles had the unique ability to chart hits in both R&B and country music.* ABOVE: *Johnny Cash, the Man in Black Leather, during a television taping in 1973.*

ABOVE: *Cash with Bob Dylan. Dylan was fascinated with Cash's music, and these two men have created some of the most enduring and important music in popular music history.* OPPOSITE: *Although always thought of as a solo artist, Johnny Cash put on elaborate live shows with many musicians and friends.*

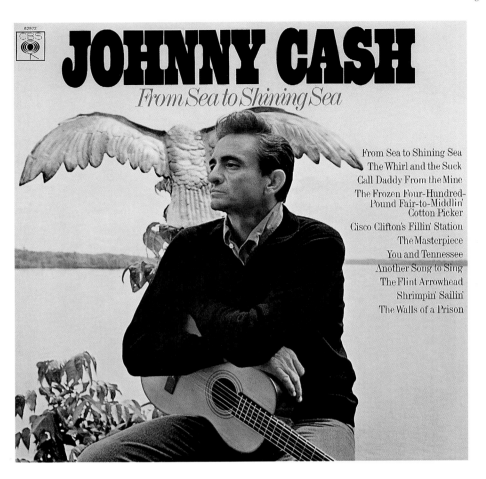

JOHNNY CASH
From Sea to Shining Sea

From Sea to Shining Sea
The Whirl and the Suck
Call Daddy From the Mine
The Frozen Four-Hundred-
Pound Fair-to-Middlin'
Cotton Picker
Cisco Clifton's Fillin' Station
The Masterpiece
You and Tennessee
Another Song to Sing
The Flint Arrowhead
Shrimpin' Sailin'
The Walls of a Prison

where other artists during Country Music Week might limit their performances to three numbers, Cash and company put on their entire show with the Carter Family, Carl Perkins, and the Statler Brothers.

Like all of the myriad fans of Johnny Cash, Clive Davis was profoundly impressed by Cash's presence.

"Johnny was a culture hero as well as a recording star," Davis wrote in his autobiography. "When he walked into a room, all eyes turned toward him; it didn't matter who else was in the room. His presence was absolutely commanding. He dressed totally in black. He is tall and powerfully built, and when he walked in your direction, you automatically stepped out of his way."

High praise indeed from a man who regularly worked with many of the greatest recording stars in the world. And Davis always made sure photographs of Cash and other famed Columbia artists were highly visible in rooms where meetings were held with new artists, their

managers, or press people. Such photos reinforced the impression of Columbia as an industry leader with the hottest recording artists signed to its roster.

But Johnny Cash was much more than just a hot recording artist. That fact was reflected by his intelligence and his continuing thirst for knowledge, and further reinforced by his tendency to pen his own liner notes and record company biographies.

In light of that, it was something of a natural progression for Johnny Cash to further develop his writing skills. Cash made his debut as an author in 1975 with *Man In Black*, a gritty and occasionally harrowing account of his own rise to fame and the price he paid to obtain it. Ending on a note of redemption—stressing Cash's renewed faith in God—*Man In Black* was as revealing and from the heart as any of the songs found in Johnny's vast catalog. And the book sold more than one million copies.

Throughout the 1970s Johnny Cash not only recorded hit singles like "Man In Black," "A Thing Called Love," "Kate," "Any Old Wind That Blows," and "One Piece at a Time," but also continued his highly personal interpretations of songs that personified America. One such release was 1972's *America: A 200-Year Salute in Story and Song*, which contained twenty-one tracks of narration—delivered in Cash's best rumbling recitation voice—alternating with songs of his country's history and legendary characters like Paul Revere, Abraham Lincoln, and Daniel Boone.

Johnny Cash further refined his "Americana" series with 1977's *The Rambler*, which again alternated dialogue with songs. Such topical explorations, in the hands of lesser artists, would come across as mawkish or strident. But in the hands of Johnny Cash, they come across as honest and forthright. Who better to tell the tales of such a large nation? As Cash himself wrote in his liner notes to 1968's *From Sea to Shining Sea:*

"From Maine to California, from the Sleepy Hollow mountain country, from Stove Pipe Wells to Tarpon Springs. The land is big. Be proud it's free."

ABOVE: *Always a trailblazer, Johnny Cash did spoken word albums like 1968's* From Sea to Shining Sea *years before the format became more common.*
OPPOSITE: *This photograph says it all, summing up the essence of an American legend: Johnny Cash, The Man in Black.*

CHAPTER 7

REDEMPTION

As the 1970s came to an end,

space must have been getting

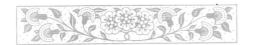

tight on the shelves of the Cash

household. After all, Johnny Cash had

been awarded a virtual pile of

BMI, Cash Box, Country Music

Association, and Grammy awards.

PAGES 90-91: *The Highwaymen onstage—four respected and justifiably honored singer/songwriter veterans—Willie Nelson, Waylon Jennings, Johnny Cash, Kris Kristofferson (left to right).* ABOVE: *Johnny and June were guests of Watergate prosecutor James Neal on November 11, 1974, during the lengthy legal proceedings in Washington.* OPPOSITE: *The former roommates, Johnny Cash and Waylon Jennings. Cash has borrowed one of Waylon's Fender Telecaster guitars for this song on a Canadian television special.*

Cash had played for presidents of the United States—democrats and republicans alike—and continued to travel around the world playing shows and cementing his stature as a musical legend. But while that reputation was fully certified, it couldn't hide a slightly disturbing fact—the hits that Johnny Cash had so regularly created seemed to be coming with less frequency. In fact, since "One Piece at a Time" began its descent from the number thirty-three position on the pop charts in May 1976, there were no more national smash hit singles featuring Cash's distinctive sound.

Some artists, however, reach a level of prestige where chart performance is no longer the means by which a career is judged. When you consider an artist like Frank Sinatra, Bob Dylan, or Tony Bennett—or

Johnny Cash—the strength of his art makes it seem almost trivial to discuss his career in terms of the cutthroat world of hit singles.

During this period, the albums of Johnny Cash still rang up consistent sales figures, and the prestige factor that Columbia president Clive Davis often referred to—where a photo of Johnny Cash could instantly reinforce the image that Columbia was the home of legends—was something difficult to equate with sales figures. But things had indeed changed behind the scenes at Columbia. In 1967, when he reached the age of sixty-five, longtime Johnny Cash producer Don Law retired from Columbia. Although it would have seemed logical for Law's coproducer, Frank Jones, to take over direction of the Cash creative efforts, Bob Johnston from the New York A&R department assumed this position when he was appointed Columbia's Director of A&R for country & western.

Johnston had sweeping plans, but he was unpopular among Nashville artists and personnel. A corporate shuffle initiated by Clive Davis in 1968 saw Johnston relegated to the title Producer at Large, while Billy Sherrill—who had been overseeing the creative responsibil-

ABOVE LEFT: *The Cash family, June, John, and Johnny, travel by bus at Frankfurt's airport during a 1972 German tour, one of Cash's many international sojourns.* ABOVE: *In Jeruselum to tape for a Christmas television special, Johnny Cash pauses to absorb the significance of the region.* OPPOSITE: *John Carter Cash hits the stage at the ripe old age of three to join his father at the Hilton in Las Vegas in May 1973.*

ABOVE: *Johnny Cash draws on the set of* A Gunfight. OPPOSITE: *Cash during filming of* A Gunfight, *looking every bit a tough inhabitant of the Old West.*

ities of Columbia's subsidiary label Epic—was assigned the executive responsibilities in Nashville for both Epic and Columbia.

As Producer at Large, though, Johnston retained Johnny Cash as one of his acts and did oversee the recording of both of the hugely successful prison live recordings. Eventually, though, Billy Sherrill, Don Law, Larry Butler, Lou Robin, Jack Clement, Rodney Crowell, Charlie Bragg, and Johnny Cash himself were among those who took producer credits at one session or another.

Many of these sessions took place at a studio that Cash himself had constructed—appropriately known as House of Cash—near his home in Hendersonville. First opened in 1972, House of Cash provided comfortable and familiar surroundings for the business of recording.

Despite all of these changes to his creative environment and the corresponding decline of his fortunes in the highly competitive world of the hit single, few musicians could hope to match Johnny Cash's global star power.

With booking agent and current Cash manager Lou Robin helping to direct international sojourns, Johnny Cash and company spent large parts of the 1970s and 1980s visiting and performing in such far-flung sites as Finland, Ireland, Hungary, Czechoslovakia, Germany, Spain, and Poland—often at times when political pressures made such treks risky propositions.

It was during one such international trip that one of Johnny Cash's first major collaborations of the 1980s took place. In April 1981, three of the legendary names from the hallowed days of Sun Records—Carl Perkins, Jerry Lee Lewis, and Johnny Cash—were all on separate tours in Germany. At Cash's show in Stuttgart on April 23, he was surprised with a visit from Lewis and Perkins, both of whom were off that night. The result was a live recording of three legends performing together, enjoying each other's company, and creating a spontaneous and highly enjoyable live album. Upon release the album bore the title *The Survivors*, which seemed entirely appropriate considering the past histories of these three men.

OPPOSITE: *Cash and his guitar have traveled the world.*   ABOVE: *Cash strikes a stoic pose in his performance attire of 1974.*

Shortly thereafter, Cash had another terrifying encounter with drugs, and he very nearly did not survive. This encounter began with, of all crazy things, an attack by an ostrich. At the time, Cash maintained a fifty-acre (20.2-hectare) area stocked with wild game, including the ostrich. While Cash was walking in his game preserve one day, the huge bird viciously launched itself at him. The violent collision and Cash's subsequent fall resulted in five broken ribs for the Man in Black—and a return to painkillers. From there, it was only a short journey to sleep-

Johnny Cash (right) and Waylon Jennings, playing on their outlaw images, pose in western garb for the cover to their collaborative album, 1986's Heroes.

ing pills and stimulants.

A broken kneecap from another fall soon after only reinforced Cash's need for painkillers, and upon returning from a European tour in 1983 Cash was hospitalized for internal bleeding—his stomach was failing from the corrosive effects of the drugs. Surgery was performed to repair the damage, but that led to a need for morphine, and in his weakened condition Johnny Cash nearly died.

As he slowly recovered from the surgery, Cash became determined to conquer his dependency on drugs once and for all. Armed with this commitment to solve his problems, Johnny entered the program at the famed Betty Ford Center.

During the darkest days after his surgery, Johnny's spirits had been buoyed by messages from his old friend and former roommate, Waylon Jennings. One of Jennings' hospital messages had simply read, "I can't imagine a world without Johnny Cash. Get out of there."

In fact, Waylon would soon play a large part in the next major chapter of Cash's career: the recordings created by The Highwayman quartet consisting of Cash, Jennings, Willie Nelson, and Kris Kristofferson.

The Highwayman project was a country music marketer's dream project. Take four of the greatest names in the history of country music, put them in the studio, and then watch the results fly up the charts. And in 1985, fly they did.

The first single, "Highwayman," featured all four performers, and was backed by a Cash-Nelson duet, "The Human Condition," designed to showcase the two most commercially popular members of the quartet. "Highwayman" entered the *Billboard* country charts in May and spent the next twenty weeks in residence. It was the first single bearing Cash's voice to reach the number one spot since June 1976, when "One Piece at a Time" had scored so well. By September the album *Highwayman* had reached the top spot on the country charts; in the end, it even broke into the top one hundred on the pop charts.

At the same time, Johnny Cash was also delving further into the word of acting and film production, fortunately with greater success than back in the days of *Five Minutes to Live*.

Willie Nelson (left) and Waylon Jennings (right), who had previously collaborated on Wanted: The Outlaws *in 1976, were joined in 1985 by Johnny Cash (second from right) and Kris Kristofferson (second from left) for the* Highwayman *album.*

Johnny and June produced a film that mixed story with song—a retelling of the life of Jesus called *Gospel Road*. Cash starred alongside Kirk Douglas in *A Gunfight* and fought against illiteracy in *The Pride of Jesse Hallam*, a film made for television. He played a driven sheriff searching for justice as he chased a chillingly despicable Andy Griffith

in 1983's *Murder in Coweta County*, a film that also featured June. And June also joined Johnny in 1986's *Last Days of Frank and Jesse James*.

While the days of *The Johnny Cash Show* were long in the past, Johnny maintained a musical presence on network television with guest appearances and shows like his mid-1980s Christmas special, with Jerry

ABOVE: *At yet another television taping, Johnny Cash sings the songs of a nation.*   OPPOSITE: *Although his record sales had slowed somewhat in the 1980s, Cash continued to tour extensively.*

Lee Lewis as guest star. The Christmas show also featured members of the Cash family, including Johnny and June's son, John Carter, who was born in 1970.

But John Carter wasn't the only member of the Cash-Carter clan with performing aspirations. June's daughter Carlene Carter broke into country music and brought a focus on rockabilly rhythms to her sounds when she was married to British bass guitarist–recording artist–producer Nick Lowe, in the process recording several strong albums. And Johnny's daughter Roseanne Cash had become one of country music's most popular and effective female vocalists.

In 1986, *Man In White*, Johnny Cash's second effort as an author, was published. This time, rather than writing part two of his autobiography, Cash took on the challenge of a novel: the story of a biblical character who had long fascinated him, the Apostle Paul. Cash had delved deeply into a religious and historical library left to him by June's late father, Ezra. In fact, since 1977 Cash had shown a particular interest in Paul and his conversion. But it took nearly ten years of fitful work before Cash finally completed *Man In White*.

Cash was aware that writing a religious novel might not be the most popular of works. In fact, in the book's introduction and acknowledgments, he wrote:

"Thanks also to the agnostics, the atheists, the unconcerned, and the uncaring. These may have been among the most inspiring and encouraging by providing the negative force I needed against my determination."

Cash also knew full well that few things can stir up controversy as quickly as religious issues. He knew that he would be questioned as to the religious viewpoint from which this tale was told, and he arrived at a complex answer—yet one that was easily summed up:

> *I finally settled on a fundamental answer. "I, as a believer that Jesus of Nazareth, a Jew, the Christ of the Greeks, was the Anointed One of God (born of the seed of David, upon faith as Abraham had faith, and it was accounted to him for righteousness), am grafted onto the true vine, and am one of the heirs of God's covenant with Israel."*

"What?"
"I'm a Christian," I said. "Don't put me in another box."

As much as Cash's foray into the realm of serious writing may have surprised his fans, perhaps an even greater shock came that same year when Cash left his record company of over twenty-five years.

It was an unsettling time in the recording industry. Columbia, once an American flagship label, had been purchased by Sony. The compact

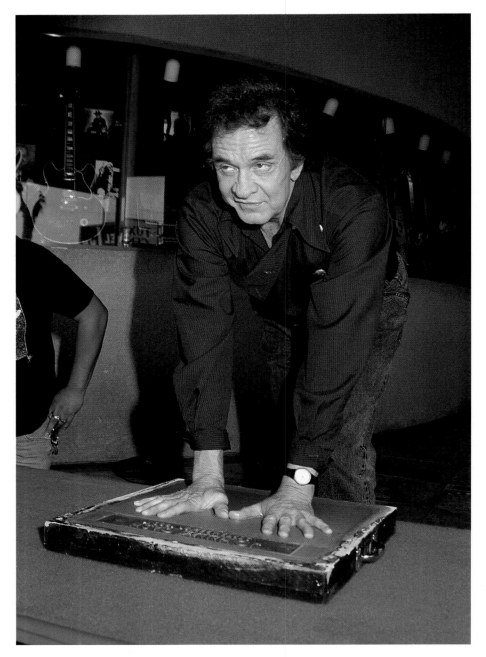

The hands of a legend, enshrined for posterity.

disc was beginning to supplant the venerable vinyl album. Johnny Cash signed with Mercury/Polygram Records in 1986 and headed back into the studio.

While the Mercury recordings didn't burn up the charts, they performed decently enough, frequently breaking into the country music top fifty. Even "Ballad of a Teenage Queen" made a return visit to the charts, this time in the guise of a duet with Johnny and his daughter Roseanne.

Johnny and June in 1996, with Cash's second title for American Recordings on the verge of release.

In 1990 *Highwayman II* was released, with Cash's voice back on the Columbia label for this recording. The album placed in the top five of the country charts, and remained listed for over six months. Its single, "Silver Stallion," performed moderately well, although it failed to make a mark on the pop charts.

By 1992 compact disc box sets providing comprehensive overviews of an artist's career were becoming hugely popular. There was little doubt that Johnny Cash—and his huge back catalog—was a perfect choice for such a project to be issued by Columbia. Thus was born *The Essential Johnny Cash*, a part of the Columbia Country Classics series.

Including fifteen of the songs Cash recorded for Sam Phillips at Sun Records, *The Essential Johnny Cash* spanned thirty years of recordings, spreading seventy-five songs over three CDs. It should come as no surprise that—as he had done so many times during his career at Columbia—Johnny Cash himself provided liner notes to help put things in perspective. He wrote in part:

> *I am proud of the 28 years I was affiliated with Columbia, or CBS, or Sony, or whatever the company chooses to be called now. The fact that Sony bought the record company, including those 28 years of my work, has taken time to get used to.*
>
> *Do they understand that it's a piece of my life, a piece of my heart, a piece of my soul? I hope so, because it is.*
>
> *A flood tide of memories come back as I scan these titles. Call it "The Essential Johnny Cash" if you will, but know this: Here is my heart. Here is my flesh and blood. Here is my spirit. There isn't one of the 75 songs that don't belong, that don't fit.*
>
> *There is a memory to go with every song…*
>
> *Believe me, this album flashes the spectrum of the total me music-wise. Each one is a piece of my life. There are many more than these, but for the time being, I'm satisfied to share this much of myself with you.*

Coinciding with the release of *The Essential Johnny Cash* in 1992, Cash received another tremendous honor—he was inducted into the

Rock and Roll Hall of Fame. There had never been any doubt that Cash's lofty place in popular music was marked clearly, but his importance was reflected by the musical peers who were selected for induction with him that year: Bobby "Blue" Bland, Booker T. and the MG's, The Jimi Hendrix Experience, The Isley Brothers, Sam and Dave, The Yardbirds, and non-performers Leo Fender, who founded and designed Fender Guitars, Bill Graham, the groundbreaking concert promoter, and Doc Pomus, who wrote classic songs like "Save the Last Dance For Me" and "Viva Las Vegas." Like Johnny Cash, all of these men had had a profound influence in shaping popular music.

With all of this retrospection, musical and otherwise, 1992 could very easily have marked the last chapter in the career of Johnny Cash. But Johnny Cash was far from done with the world of music. He may have justifiably been celebrated as a legend, but one of the qualities that made him legendary was a continuous evolution. In 1993, that evolu-

ABOVE LEFT: *Grammy Legend Award in hand, Johnny Cash is joined by his family after being honored during the 1990 awards ceremony of the National Academy of Recording Arts and Sciences. Son John Carter Cash, wife June Carter Cash, Johnny, daughter Roseanne Cash, and Roseanne's husband (at the time) Rodney Crowell (left to right) share in the happiness.* ABOVE RIGHT: *June Carter Cash and Johnny Cash backstage in 1989.*

Cash with Tom Petty. Petty and his band, the Heartbreakers, backed Cash on his Unchained *release in 1996.*

tion took its next step when Johnny Cash signed with Rick Rubin's American Recordings label.

Rubin had gained a strong reputation after starting the Def Jam label with Russell Simmons and producing a number of influential recordings in the 1980s. He had a talent for navigating the treacherous waters of a music industry still unsettled by the onslaught of punk rock in the late 1970s and the conversion to compact disc less than ten years later.

Johnny Cash recording at home in 1994, refining the songs that revitalized his career on his new record label, American Recordings.

Cash trades licks with famed guitarists Steve Cropper (second from right) and the Rolling Stones' Keith Richards (right) at the Rock and Roll Hall of Fame induction ceremony jam.

When Rubin decided to split with Simmons to start his own record label—originally known as Def American Recordings before being changed to plain American Recordings—it was not a particularly shocking move. After all, there were a lot of young artists and bands who were more than willing to follow the young producer into uncharted territory. But to sign a legend like Johnny Cash?

"I think we have a very cool roster for a young label, great acts, but very little history," Rubin said at the time. "Conceptually, for a baby label to have a legendary artist to work with is a very exciting thing.

"Johnny Cash is this historic, legendary, outlaw figure," Rubin continued. "Outlaw is part of what I perceive this label to be about. That's the essence of rock and roll, and Johnny Cash clearly fits into that rebel mentality. All of our acts to a certain degree are outsiders. John will tell

AN UNLIKELY SAVIOR

If ever there seemed to be an unlikely candidate to bring redemption to the career of Johnny Cash, it was Rick Rubin. But with the signing of Johnny Cash to Rubin's American Recordings label in 1993, the maverick producer began the process of reestablishing Johnny Cash as one of the most important recording artists of the 1990s.

Rick Rubin began the road to recording industry respect in the humblest of surroundings: his dorm room at New York University. It was there that he founded Def Jam Records with his partner Russell Simmons. The young Rubin built an empire by seeing the potential of merging rock with rap, and he oversaw such significant projects as the Run DMC and Aerosmith collaboration on "Walk This Way" and the Beastie Boys' influential *Licensed to Ill.*

In 1987 Rubin and Simmons split, with the result being the birth of Rubin's new Def American Recordings after Rick relocated to the West Coast. In the years since the founding of Def American Recordings—and the subsequent name change to American Recordings—Rubin's label has presented music by a wide array of intriguing artists, ranging from the metallic fury of Slayer to the hard country-boogie of Raging Slab. And Rubin has kept busy producing acts such as AC/DC, Red Hot Chili Peppers, The Cult, and Tom Petty for other labels.

With such a wide array of musical interests and a reputation for successful sonic experimentation, perhaps the alliance with Johnny Cash really was just a logical next step in the career of Rick Rubin.

"To me, for his first record, the idea of Johnny Cash by himself seems right," Rubin said of the stripped-down production on Cash's *American Recordings.* "I felt it would be a healthy reintroduction to the mainstream. Often when a legendary artist works with a lot of other well known people, the focus of the project shifts. I think we made a brutally honest record."

Johnny and his new producer, Rick Rubin, the founder of American Recordings.

ABOVE : *Entering a new era of his career, Johnny Cash in 1994 was about to find himself popular with a new generation.*   OPPOSITE: *The cover of Johnny's strong-selling 1994 release, the recording that exposed thousands of young listeners to the wonders of Cash.*

you that from the beginning of his career he's always been an outsider of the mainstream. He's always done things the way he's wanted to do them and he's had great success doing it on his own terms."

Signing Cash was one thing—but what to do with him once it was time to record? Rubin had a brilliant but simple idea. Focus on three things—Johnny Cash's voice, his guitar, and strong songs. Rubin figured that was all he needed, and Cash agreed.

"I've always wanted to do an album that was Johnny Cash alone— that's the concept," Cash said. "This is what I've always wanted to do, and I was able to do it with Rick. Making records over the years, I've experienced a great deal of frustrations, overproduction and all that jazz. To be able to sit down with a tape that I'm proud of is just great."

Cash and Rubin first began recording in May 1993, often holding the sessions in the living room of Rubin's California home. Over the next several months, Johnny Cash recorded scores of songs, many of them written by musicians far removed from the country music world. People like Tom Waits, Glenn Danzig, and Billy Gibbons of ZZ Top all had songs recorded and considered by Cash and Rubin for inclusion on the album.

When *American Recordings* was released late in the spring of 1994, the stark recording was met with rave reviews and tumultuous praise. Suddenly, at the age of sixty-two, Johnny Cash was the hippest recording artist around.

"I don't think I ever worked so well with a producer in my entire career," Cash said when the album was released. "Rick came up with some songs that I thought were so far out of left field and such weird ideas for me to do. I'm talking about traditional, classic, western, folk, and country songs. Now that we've done them, they feel so right. Working with Rick, all of the experimenting, kind of spread me out and expanded my range of material. This is the best I can do as an artist, as a solo artist, this is it."

Johnny Cash continued to work the road in support of his new album, both with the large Johnny Cash Show that has pleased audiences for decades and with a new, more intimate show that focuses on the atmospheric strengths displayed on *American Recordings.*

In 1996, Johnny Cash and Rick Rubin were back at work putting the finishing touches on Cash's second release for the American Recordings label. With the goal of fleshing out the sound while still retaining the open feel of its predecessor, *Unchained's* sessions included recordings of songs like Soundgarden's "Rusty Cage" with Cash backed this time by Tom Petty and the Heartbreakers.

"Making this album is the greatest experience I've ever had with a producer," Cash enthused in the summer of 1996. "This record we're doing now is the most in-depth relationship I've had with a producer in sitting down eye-to-eye and tooth-to-tooth and working out the songs and deciding which ones to do. I think I have enjoyed working with Rick more on this album than any album I've ever done."

Of course, there could well be many more albums yet to come. Johnny Cash's career has covered much ground—there's no denying that. But it seems more true than ever that a man as complex, as thoughtful, as honest, and as feeling as Johnny Cash will always have something more to offer to enrich the lives of his listeners.

It was in recognition of the achievements of Johnny Cash that an announcement was made in September 1996 that Cash would be honored at the Kennedy Center in Washington, D.C., for his many contributions to the nation's culture.

In a modern world of the Internet and instantaneous communication, the songs of Johnny Cash—any one of them—hark back to times that called for a different means of passing the word or telling a tale.

And although Johnny Cash, standing alone with his acoustic guitar and rumbling voice, may be the very definition of low-tech, his musical messages and their means of conveyance connect with the human spirit on a level that pure technology will never surpass.

OPPOSITE: *Cash's face reflects the troubled times he has weathered, but his rugged countenance only makes his songs seem more believable and heartfelt.*

DISCOGRAPHY

When an artist is as important and prolific as Johnny Cash—and has a career spanning more than four decades—the sheer number of recorded releases and recording sessions alone could be the subject of a book. In fact, Cash historian John L. Smith has turned this subject into three excellent books for the aid of music historians and devoted fans. Detailing Cash's sessions, musicians, chart positions, and release dates, the two discographies listed under this book's bibliography—along with their companion volume *The Johnny Cash Recording Catalog* (Greenwood Press)—provide a sure path through the maze of Johnny Cash's recorded works.

For the listener interested in a manageable overview of the career of Johnny Cash, three compact disc releases are recommended:

The Essential Johnny Cash 1955–1983 (1992)
Johnny Cash at Folsom Prison and San Quentin (1990)
Wanted Man (1994)

The Essential Johnny Cash, released by Columbia, contains three CDs scanning Cash's Sun and CBS works, while both of the landmark live prison recordings are combined on the Columbia release *Johnny Cash at Folsom Prison and San Quentin*. *Wanted Man* collects the best of his association with Mercury Records from 1986 until 1992.

For those who wish to delve deeper into Johnny Cash's 1950s and 1960s recordings, the following box sets from the German label Bear Family Records gather together nearly every studio recording Cash made during those decades, and add a number of session outtakes and unreleased recordings as well:

The Man In Black 1954–1958 (1990)
The Man In Black 1959–1962 (1991)
The Man In Black 1963–1969 Plus (1995)
Come Along and Ride This Train (1991)

Although there have been numerous Cash albums of varied quality released on dozens of record labels, the following full-length albums make up the main body of Cash's recorded work.

Sun Records
Johnny Cash with His Hot and Blue Guitar (1957)
Johnny Cash Sings the Songs that Made Him Famous (1958)
Johnny Cash Sings Hank Williams and Other Favorite Tunes (1960)
Now Here's Johnny Cash (1961)
All Aboard the Blue Train (1963)
Get Rhythm (1969)
Showtime (1969)
Story Songs of the Trains and Rivers (1969)
The Singing Story Teller (1970)

Columbia Records

The Fabulous Johnny Cash (1958)

Hymns by Johnny Cash (1959)

Songs of Our Soil (1959)

Now There Was a Song (1960)

Ride This Train (1960)

Hymns from the Heart (1962)

The Sound of Johnny Cash (1962)

Blood, Sweat and Tears (1963)

Ring of Fire (1963)

The Christmas Spirit (1963)

Keep On the Sunny Side (with the Carter Family, 1964)

I Walk the Line (1964)

Bitter Tears (Ballads of the American Indian) (1964)

Orange Blossom Special (1965)

Ballads of the True West (1965)

Mean as Hell (1965)

The Sons of Katie Elder (soundtrack, 1965)

Everybody Loves a Nut (1966)

Happiness Is You (1966)

Carryin' On (with June Carter, 1967)

From Sea to Shining Sea (1968)

Johnny Cash at Folsom Prison (1968)

The Holy Land (1969)

Johnny Cash at San Quentin (1969)

Hello I'm Johnny Cash (1970)

The Johnny Cash Show (1970)

I Walk the Line (soundtrack, 1970)

Man in Black (1971)

A Thing Called Love (1972)

Johnny Cash Family Christmas (1972)

America (A 200-Year Salute in Story and Song) (1972)

The Gospel Road (1973)

Any Old Wind that Blows (1973)

Johnny Cash and His Woman (with June Carter, 1973)

The Junkie and the Juicehead Minus Me (1974)

Ragged Old Flag (1974)

John R. Cash (1975)

Look at Them Beans (1975)

The Johnny Cash Children's Album (1975)

Strawberry Cake (1976)

One Piece at a Time (1976)

The Last Gunfighter Ballad (1977)

The Rambler (1977)

Gone Girl (1978)

I Would Like to See You Again (1978)

Silver (1979)

Rockabilly Blues (1980)

The Baron (1981)

The Survivors (with Jerry Lee Lewis and Carl Perkins, 1982)

The Adventures of Johnny Cash (1982)

Johnny 99 (1983)

Rainbow (1985)

Highwayman (with Kris Kristofferson, Waylon Jennings, and Willie Nelson; 1985)

Heroes (with Waylon Jennings, 1986)

Highwayman 2 (with Kris Kristofferson, Waylon Jennings, and Willie Nelson; 1990)

Mercury

Johnny Cash Is Coming to Town (1987)

Water From the Wells of Home (1988)

Boom Chicka Boom (1989)

The Mystery of Life (1991)

American Recordings

American Recordings (1994)

Unchained (1996)

INDEX

PHOTOGRAPHY CREDITS

Courtesy of American Recordings: p. 109

AP/Wide World Photos: pp. 62 top left, 64, 82 left, 92, 101

Archive Photos: pp. 59, 68, 72, 76, 80

©**Frank Driggs Collection**: pp. 56–57, 63 bottom

Everett Collection: pp. 20, 46, 62 top right, 63 top, 75, 83–85, 87, 98, 102, ©Leigh Wiener: 86

©**Ron Galella**: p. 105

Globe Photos: pp. 70–71, ©Camera Press: 90, ©John Barrett: 108 left

Michael Ochs Archives: Front endpaper, pp. 6, 8–9, 11–12, 15, 21–23, 24 right, 27, 29 both, 32, 36, 38, 41–44, 47–48, 58, 60 both, 66, 67 right, ©BMI: 10, 62 bottom

Personality Photos, Inc.: pp. 7 all, 82 right

Photofest: pp. 13, 67 left, 74, 93–95 left, 97

Retna Ltd.: ©David Redfern: p. 78, ©Camera Press: pp. 79, ©Gary Gershoff: 103, ©M. Bourquard: 104, ©Steve Granitz: 106 right, 107, ©Beth Gwinn: 108 right, 111, ©Camera Press/Peter MacDiarmid: 113, ©Beth Gwinn/Retna Ltd. back endpaper

Courtesy of Showtime Archives, Toronto: pp. 2, 14, 16–17, 33, 52 both, 88–89, 96, 99-100, 114, ©Colin Escott: 24, 28, 30, 34–35, 37, 40, 49, 51, 53, 55, 61, 73, ©Colin Escott/Elmer Williams: 31, ©Colin Escott/G. Hardy: 39, ©Lynn Russwurm: 45, 54, ©American Recordings: 110

UPI/Corbis-Bettmann: pp. 18, 50, 65, 69, 77, 81, 95 right, Reuters/Corbis-Bettmann: p.106 left

BIBLIOGRAPHY

Allen, Bob. *Come Along and Ride This Train*. Hambergen, Germany: Bear Family Records, 1991.

Cash, Johnny. *Man In Black*. New York: Warner Books, 1975.

———. *Man In White*. San Francisco: Harper & Row, 1986.

———. *Songs of Johnny Cash*. New York: Dial Press, 1970.

Cash, June Carter. *From the Heart*. New York: St. Martin's Press, 1987.

Davis, Clive. *Clive: Inside the Record Business*. New York: Ballantine Books, 1976.

Escott, Colin. *The Man In Black 1954–1958*. Hambergen, Germany: Bear Family Records, 1990.

———. *The Man In Black 1959–1962*. Hambergen, Germany: Bear Family Records, 1991.

———. *The Man In Black 1963–1969 Plus*. Hambergen, Germany: Bear Family Records, 1995.

Malone, Bill C. *Country Music USA*. Austin: University of Texas Press, 1985.

Nite, Norm N. *Rock On Almanac: The First Four Decades of Rock 'n' Roll*. New York: HarperCollins, 1992.

Smith, John L. *The Johnny Cash Discography 1954–1983*. Westport, CT: Greenwood Press, 1985.

———. *The Johnny Cash Discography 1984–1993*. Westport, CT: Greenwood Press 1994.

Various. "The Remarkable Journey of Johnny Cash: 35th Anniversary." *Billboard Magazine*, 1990.

Wren, Christopher S. *Winners Got Scars Too: The Life and Legends of Johnny Cash*. New York: Dial Press, 1971.